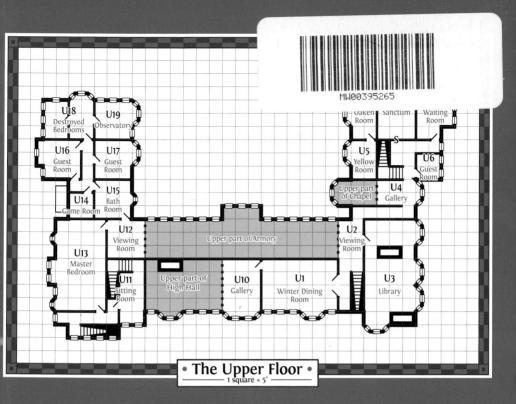

• The Upper Floor •
— 1 square = 5' —

U18 Destroyed Bedrooms
U19 Observatory
U16 Guest Room
U17 Guest Room
U14 Game Room
U15 Bath Room
U13 Master Bedroom
U12 Viewing Room
U11 Sitting Room
Upper part of High Hall
Upper part of Armory
U10 Gallery
U1 Winter Dining Room
U2 Viewing Room
Oaken Room
Sanctum
Waiting Room
U5 Yellow Room
U6 Guest Room
Upper part of Chapel
U4 Gallery
U3 Library

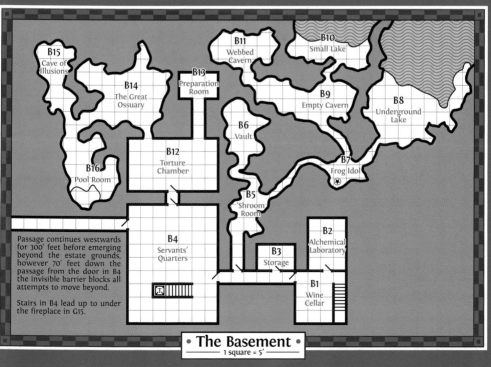

• The Basement •
— 1 square = 5' —

B15 Cave of Illusions
B14 The Great Ossuary
B13 Preparation Room
B11 Webbed Cavern
B10 Small Lake
B9 Empty Cavern
B8 Underground Lake
B6 Vault
B12 Torture Chamber
B16 Pool Room
B7 Frog Idol
B5 'Shroom Room
B4 Servants' Quarters
B3 Storage
B2 Alchemical Laboratory
B1 Wine Cellar

Passage continues westwards for 300' feet before emerging beyond the estate grounds, however 70' feet down the passage from the door in B4 the invisible barrier blocks all attempts to move beyond.

Stairs in B4 lead up to under the fireplace in G15.

NON OMNIS MORIAR

the cursed chateau

Writing
James Maliszewski

Cover Art
Yannick Bouchard

Graphic Design and Interior Art
Jez Gordon

Editing
Craig Judd

Text © James Maliszewski 2016. Issued Under Exclusive License to:

LAMENTATIONS
of the
FLAME PRINCESS

www.lotfp.com

ISBN Print 978-952-5904-96-3   ISBN PDF 978-952-5904-97-0
Printed in Finland by Otava Book Printing Ltd, Keuruu 2016
EXPANDED EDITION — FIRST PRINTING: 2000 COPIES

dedication

This adventure is dedicated
to the memories of
Bob Bledsaw, Tom Moldvay,
and Clark Ashton Smith,
all of whom excited my
youthful imagination
in ways I can never
hope to calculate.

contents

tables

introduction

AUNTED HOUSES HAVE fascinated me since I was a child. In part, that's a consequence of my growing up in the 1970s, a decade awash in horror and the occult. It was also the decade that brought us movies like *The House That Dripped Blood, The Legend of Hell House, Burnt Offerings,* and of course *The Amityville Horror*—none of which I actually saw until years later, but about which I had heard many second-hand tales from older neighborhood kids as well as from the proverbial cousins of my friends, who clearly had very lenient and open-minded parents, if even half the stories about what they were allowed to do are to be believed.

THE CURSED CHATEAU is my attempt to present a haunted house like the ones I imagined in my childhood, as seen through the lens of old-school fantasy roleplaying games. Consequently, the chateau is something of a "fun house," a term used to describe a style of early RPG adventure exemplified by modules like *Tegel Manor* (written by Bob Bledsaw and published in 1977 by Judges Guild) and *Castle Amber* (written by Tom Moldvay and published in 1981 by TSR). Depending on one's perspective, a fun house is either "whimsical" or "nonsensical," in that its inhabitants and locations show some degree of randomness.

One room might contain nothing more than some dusty furniture while the one right next to it is a raucous spectral dinner party whose participants encourage the Player Characters to join them, and the one right next to that is home to a collection of skeletons dancing to music no one but they can hear.

In a fun house, there's often no way to determine what lurks behind the next door or down a nearby corridor and that fact irritates some players who value naturalism and rationality even in their fantasy. Without it, they argue, it's difficult, if not impossible, to plan ahead or think strategically and thereby minimize the likelihood of their characters suffering some terrible fate. I'm sympathetic to this perspective and, in general, my adventure locales are fairly reasonable, even orderly places that "make sense"—which is precisely why a place like the chateau makes for a good change of pace!

One of the reasons I liked stories of haunted houses as a child was because haunted houses defied logic. The creepy things that supposedly happened inside them—disembodied voices, bleeding walls, apparitions—represented incursions of the weird and the supernatural into our humdrum existence. They were frightening precisely because they followed their own rules rather than those of the rational, scientific, mechanical world we believe ourselves to inhabit. To my mind, that's what a fun house adventure locale does, too: it breaks the rules of the game and does its own thing.

Consequently, **THE CURSED CHATEAU**, like most fun houses, is a difficult adventure. The titular curse under which the chateau has fallen literally changes the rules of *Lamentations of the Flame Princess* in various ways, both subtle and obvious. These changes punish certain types of behavior and reward others. Players who either fail to grasp the nature of the curse or who choose to act against that nature will soon find their characters suffering under great disadvantages. This is by design. At the same time, the chateau and its inhabitants aren't wholly devoid of meaning. There are clues, hints, and information scattered about that perceptive and patient players may discover so as to make their characters' explorations less deadly. Such players may even see their characters escape the chateau not only alive but also richer and wiser.

THE CURSED CHATEAU existed in two versions prior to the present one. The original version was submitted to the *Fight On!/Otherworld Miniatures Adventure Contest* in the summer of 2008, where it won Honorable Mention. A slightly expanded version was later published in 2009 as a separate product. The version you now hold in your hands is much larger than either of the two previous versions and contains many changes and expansions. Some of these changes were necessitated by the default historical setting of *Lamentations of the Flame Princess*; others were the result of years of having run the adventure myself and listening to the feedback of others who did so as well. It is hoped that this latest version will be as well received as its predecessors.

— James Maliszewski

background

 ORD JOUDAIN AYARAI was the scion of a long line of aristocrats in the remote province of France known as Averenha in the local Occitan dialect. His family had been wealthy and influential for longer than any could remember. An only child, his parents died when he was four years old, entrusting him to older relatives and servants, who cared for his education and upbringing. A precocious, charming boy, Lord Joudain matured first into a vain, dissolute youth and then a jaded, venal adult. He had the power, money, and influence to satisfy his every desire and did so—but it was not enough to overcome his ennui.

Lord Joudain turned to necromancy, black magic, and eventually devilry as means to alleviate his world-weariness and boredom. He communed with elemental entities, slew his servants and raised them from the dead, and even summoned demons from Beyond, but he found no pleasure in any of these activities. Lord Joudain eventually came to the conclusion that the mortal realm offered him nothing but tedium and so committed suicide according to a ritual found in an ancient grimoire in the hope that the next world might prove more interesting than the present one.

Lord Joudain's consciousness persisted after his death, just as he had hoped. Rather than moving on to some other plane of existence—or even the heaven, hell, or purgatory preached by the Church—his being was instead bound to his earthly home for reasons he had neither anticipated nor could explain. He could not move on to whatever reward—or punishment—awaited him in some afterlife. Instead, he remained forever linked to his chateau.

Unable to manifest himself in a visible form for long, Lord Joudain can, however, influence events within his old home and command his now-undead servants (see Joudain's Fun, below). He can also create a magical barrier that prevents entrance to and egress from the chateau's grounds. This last ability is the primary way Lord Joudain now seeks to entertain himself: trapping foolhardy travelers and tormenting them. As soon as the characters enter the grounds of the chateau, they are Joudain's prisoners and he intends to make full use of them for his own purposes.

involving the characters

DEPENDING ON HOW the Referee intends to use this adventure, the characters can become involved in several ways. First, they may simply stumble upon the chateau while traveling through Averenha and then enter it, unaware of its curse. Second, the characters may have heard tales of the chateau, Lord Joudain, or the curse affecting both and seek it out to see for themselves. Finally, a distant relative of Lord Joudain might employ the characters to explore the chateau so that she might lay claim to an inheritance. Other possibilities exist, of course, and the Referee is encouraged to use the chateau and its inhabitants in any way that best fits the current needs of his campaign.

random events

THOUGH DEAD, LORD Joudain is still bored. He seeks diversion and (he hopes) release from his earthly bondage by toying with any living beings who enter the ruins of his former home. Unfortunately, Joudain has become, if anything, even more fickle and malicious in death than he was in life. Just what he believes will divert him from his own suffering at any given time is thus seemingly random, at least as far as outsiders are concerned.

Every time the characters enter a keyed area — even one they have previously explored — roll once on the following Random Events table (p.10 to 13) and apply the event. Some of the possible events are repeatable and others are not. If the same non-repeatable event is rolled more than once, use the next non-repeatable event on the list. For example, the Referee rolls 1d100 and gets 21, an event that has already occurred. Instead, he goes down the list to the next non-repeatable event he has not previously rolled (in this case 24) and uses that one. The same thing happens if the event refers to an encounter with one of the household staff (see p.15) who has been destroyed. Most of the events are written in a broad enough fashion so as to be usable in any keyed area of the chateau and the surrounding areas, but the Referee is encouraged to make whatever alterations or substitutions are necessary so that the event "fits" the characters' current whereabouts. Referee modification is especially necessary in the hedge maze (see p.32), as it is an outdoor area without doors, windows, etc.

These random events are a vital part of running this adventure, which is why the table below has so many entries. The chateau is a strange, creepy, and, at times, whimsical place, and the entries below reflect that. If so desired, the Referee can replace some of the entries with ones of his own devising. Anything that might occur in a horror movie or haunted house is appropriate—but so is anything odd, peculiar, or even funny. Joudain's consciousness has been bound to the chateau for decades now and he has gone quite mad in his efforts to free himself. Who knows what peculiar happenings he might bring into being in a desperate attempt to entertain himself?

d100 RANDOM EVENT (1-25)

1. A deck of playing cards appears on a nearby table or shelf (or on the ground, if outside). The cards are stained with fresh blood.

2. A character looking into any nearby reflective surface (a mirror, window, water, etc.) sees not her own face but a red-skinned demonic one instead.

3. A statue, painting, or other work of art speaks the name of a random character and tells her, "Flee, while you still can!"

4. The characters hear disembodied cackling coming from behind the closest door or wall.

5. A colony of bats flies about the characters' heads but disappears into thin air before it reaches them.

6. The closest door suddenly swings open with a loud bang. Re-roll if there are no doors nearby.

7. The character briefly feels as if dozens of crawling insects have gotten under her clothing or armor, when in fact no such thing has occurred.

8. The next step a random character takes causes a black slimy substance to bubble out on to the surrounding area from beneath the ground/floor. The slime is not dangerous but it has a noxious odor. This event cannot occur on the upper level of the chateau, in which case nothing happens.

9. One of Lord Joudain's dogs (see p.43) wanders into the area, barks loudly, and then attacks the nearest character.

10. Hervisse (see p.19) walks in the direction of the chateau's kitchen (area L6). He takes no notice of the characters unless they impede his progress in any way.

11. Landri (see p.20) appears and says to the characters, "Can't you follow directions? The stables are that way." He then waits to see that the characters actually leave the chateau (he will open even a magically locked door) before heading toward his room. If the characters do not leave or attack him, he will call for Jaume and Miqèl (see p.19) to deal with them. Re-roll if already outside the chateau.

12. Rixenda (see p.22) crosses the characters' path. She stops to ask if the characters have seen Ysabel, as "the Master wants her." The characters' response to her (including its truthfulness) does not matter and she will head toward the high hall (see area G15) afterward.

13. The character with the lowest Charisma feels herself shoved from behind by an invisible force. She must make a saving throw versus Magic or stumble to the ground, taking no damage.

14. Ysabel (see p.23) can be seen crying in the corner of the area. She will not say anything to the characters and, if approached, will fade out of view.

15. Guilhèm (see p.18) appears. He simply smiles at the characters before proceeding away from them and fading out of view. If attacked or impeded, he calls on Jaume and Miqèl (see p.19) to aid him.

16. The character with the most experience points suddenly notices that an item is no longer on her person. A quick scan of the area reveals that the item is located nearby but with no indication whatsoever as to how it got where it is now.

17. Laurensa (see p.21) and Rixenda (see p.22) both run at the characters, attacking them.

18. Arnaud (see p.16) stomps loudly through the area, heading to Landri's chambers (area G5).

19. Any Clerics present find that their holy symbols have disappeared. The symbols will be found in the next area the characters enter.

20. Bertrand (see p.16) appears, asking the characters to hide him from Martin, who is apparently very upset with the way he has been shirking his duties. If the characters make an effort to help Bertrand, he will disappear shortly afterward. If they do not, he will first plead with them and then fly into a rage and attack them.

21. Jaume (see p.19) appears, offering to show the characters to whatever area they next wish to visit. He refrains from answering most questions, saying "That's not for me to say, madam (or sir)." He will defend himself if attacked but will otherwise not interact with the characters beyond the specific task they have given him.

22. Estève (see p.18) appears and offers to escort the characters to the high hall (area G15), where Laurensa and Rixenda await (assuming they have not been destroyed) to attack and devour them.

23. Clareta (see p.17) moves into view, cleaning and generally straightening the area. She will ask the characters to leave the area until she is done. If they do not comply, she will summon Jaume and Miqèl (see p.19) to handle the matter for her.

24. The door knob of the room turns into a tooth-filled mouth and bites the character who touches it, dealing 1d4 points of damage. If there is no door, nothing happens.

25. Guilhèm comes running at the characters, laughing happily. He simply passes through them before disappearing completely.

d100 RANDOM EVENT (26-48)

26. Miqèl (see p.19) appears, offering to lead the characters into the next area. He will defend himself if he is attacked but will otherwise not interact with the characters beyond the performance of his duties.

27. A spectral hand reaches up and tries to grab the ankle of the character with the lowest Strength. This is successful if the character fails a saving throw versus Paralyzation. The grab deals 1d4 damage and holds the character until she (or another character) attempts to break the hand's hold, after which the hand disperses.

28. A dagger flies at the first character to enter the area. Treat the dagger as a 3rd-level Fighter for determining its chance to hit. If successful, it deals normal damage, after which it is a perfectly normal dagger.

29. Mondette (see p.22) is heading toward the kitchen (area G6). She scowls at the characters as she goes by, but otherwise takes no notice of them. If attacked, she calls on Hervisse (see p.19) to protect her, but he never arrives.

30. If the area has any windows, they audibly crack and shatter, sending shards flying everywhere. The shards deal 1d6 damage to anyone within 5 feet who fails a saving throw versus Breath Weapon. Should the characters ever return to this room, the window will no longer be broken.

31. Landri (see p.20) appears, carrying a book in one hand. He gives the book to one of the characters, saying, "The Master wants you to read this before dinner this evening" before he departs. The book is, however, completely blank.

32. The characters hear a female voice say, "I thought you didn't like uninvited guests."

33. The closest nearby fireplace suddenly roars to life. The flames are real and last until they run out of fuel (1d4 Turns) or they are exting-uished. If there are no fireplaces nearby, re-roll.

34. The character with the lowest Constitution score levitates 2 feet off the ground for the number of Rounds by which her score is lower than 13, after which she simply falls to the ground. If all the characters' Constitution scores are 13 or greater, nothing happens.

35. The area is affected by magical spiderwebs that require 2d4 Turns to cut through, though flames will destroy them in 2d4 Rounds.

36. Jaume (see p.19) walks into view, smiling and muttering to himself, "It was still worth it." If no one attacks him or impedes him, he will continue to walk away.

37. Miqèl (see p.19) wanders into the area, clutching his split head and moaning through his bifurcated mouth. He completely ignores the characters unless they attack him or otherwise impede his movement.

38. The lowest-level character is pushed from behind. She must make a successful saving throw versus Paralyzation or fall to the ground.

39. A voice can be heard whispering the words to the "Our Father" in Latin but backwards.

40. Bertrand (see p.16) is found sleeping in the next area. If he is awakened, either on purpose or by making loud noises, he will be fly into a rage and attack the characters.

41. The shadow of the character with the lowest Charisma score begins to notice-ably distort and take on other shapes, including that of a horned demon, before it returns to its original shape.

42. An insubstantial cat crosses in front of the characters' path before disappearing. The first character to walk beyond where the cat appeared suffers a -1 penalty on her next saving throw.

43. A bag of 100sp appears on the floor.

44. Mondette (see p.22) appears and begins to flirt with the male character with the highest Charisma. 1d4 Rounds later, Hervisse (see p.19) will appear and attack the object of Mondette's affections. She will join in this attack with glee.

45. Fresh flowers are found in a vase on a table or shelf in the area.

46. Julian (see p.20) clomps loudly through the area. His spectral shoes appear to be covered in mud, which he tracks onto the ground. Shortly after he steps forward, he looks down, notices the mess he is making and curses to himself. He looks at the characters and says, "The Master will not like this one bit" before disappearing.

47. Hervisse (see p.19) enters the area, armed with a cleaver. He asks the characters if they have seen Mondette and "that bastard." If they hesitate to answer or question him, he begins to accuse them of "trying to hide the truth from me," after which he attacks.

48. A water-damaged book is found. The book is missing many pages and the handwriting inside is often smeared. However, it is clearly Joudain's journal. The legible pages (all of which are near the end) talk about Joudain's looking forward to seeing the latest pair of peasants whom Martin (see p.21) has brought to the chateau. He hopes that they might prove useful in his experiments.

d100 RANDOM EVENT (49-70)

49. Guilhèm (see p.18) wanders around nearby, as if searching for something. He is missing one of his shoes and asks the characters if they have seen it. If they have (see entry 78) and can direct him toward its location (or, better yet, give it to him), he will reward them by answering truthfully any one question they have about the chateau. The Referee should bear in mind that Guilhèm has the mind of a child and Joudain shielded him from many of the worst aspects of the place.

50. A piece of crumpled paper appears on the ground. If read, it is revealed to be a page from Joudain's journal in which he rants at length about his boredom and how he wishes to be entertained. He then lists several mundane activities in which he has recently engaged that he hoped might do so—reading, going riding, visiting a nearby town, etc.—but that have failed to hold his attention. He then intimates that he might need to look elsewhere for diversion.

51. Elias (see p.17) calls to the characters from behind the closest door, asking them to unlock it. The characters will find the door unlocked, despite Elias's claims. If the door is opened, he thanks the characters before heading away from them, muttering about how he will have to report Jaume and Miqèl's tomfoolery to the Master. If there are no doors nearby, nothing happens.

52. Clareta (see p.17) offers the characters some sweets from a bag that she pulls from her apron. If the characters do not accept her offer, she attacks them. If they do accept, she will wait until one or more of them has consumed the sweets before leaving. Each character who consumes one must make a saving throw versus Poison. Those who fail suffer nausea for the next 1d4 Turns, which exacts a -2 penalty on all attack rolls and saving throws. Those who succeed gain a +2 bonus to the same rolls for the same duration.

53. Any Player Characters slain in the chateau thus far are reanimated, as described on p.25. (Repeatable)

54. Nothing happens—the Player Characters get lucky this time. (Repeatable)

55. Lord Joudain briefly manifests as a ghostly apparition of himself as a child (see area G17 for a description), points at a random character, and laughs before he fades away. (Repeatable)

56. The characters hear a loud creaking noise, either beneath their own feet or above their heads, as appropriate. (Repeatable)

57. The characters hear a woman scream. (Repeatable)

58. Fresh blood drips from a nearby wall and pools on the floor. (Repeatable)

59. A broom, rake, shovel, or other similar implement springs to life briefly and smacks a nearby character on the head. The implement has Armor 13, 1 Hit Die, 5 hit points, deals 1 point of damage per hit and continues until it is destroyed. (Repeatable)

60. A skeleton assembles out of a nearby pile of bones and attacks the characters. The skeleton has Armor 14, 1 Hit Die, 4hp, and does 1d4 damage. (Repeatable)

61. Lord Joudain briefly manifests as a ghostly apparition of himself as an adult (see area G17 on the ground level for a description), stares intently at a random character and sighs deeply, before he fades away. (Repeatable)

62. The characters see glowing red eyes in the nearest darkened area. The eyes fade from view as soon as the characters get within 10 feet of them. (Repeatable)

63. A number of dancing, purplish lights appear and briefly circle about the characters before winking out of existence. (Repeatable)

64. The character with the lowest Wisdom hears her name whispered in her right ear. (Repeatable)

65. A nearby piece of furniture (or statue or bush) moves a couple of inches along the floor. (Repeatable)

66. A candle, chandelier, lantern, or other light source in the room lights itself up and remains illuminated for 1d10 Rounds before extinguishing. (Repeatable)

67. Lord Joudain briefly manifests as a ghostly apparition of himself as a youth (see area G17 on the ground level for a description), and lunges at a random character with a spectral sword, which passes right through her, before he fades away. (Repeatable)

68. A scratching sound emanates from a nearby wooden wall panel. The sound stops as soon as the characters get close to it. (Repeatable)

69. Any sources of illumination the characters are carrying (torches, lanterns, etc.) flicker for a moment and then go out. (Repeatable)

70. The character with the fewest experience points feels something move past her feet, like an animal. Looking down, she sees nothing. (Repeatable).

d100 RANDOM EVENT (71-100)

71. A small nearby object slides across the surface on which it is currently placed. (Repeatable)

72. The air temperature noticeably drops for a few seconds. (Repeatable)

73. One of the characters sees a vaguely humanoid shape out of the corner of her eye. When she turns to look at it, there is nothing there. (Repeatable)

74. The characters can hear the harpsichord begin to play. The sound seems to be emanating from the ground floor of the chateau. (Repeatable)

75. The door through which the characters just entered slams shut and is affected by *Wizard Lock* for 1d4 Turns. If there are no doors nearby, nothing happens. (Repeatable)

76. The air is suffused with a pleasant aroma not unlike lilacs. (Repeatable)

77. The character with the lowest Constitution feels an invisible hand cover her mouth and nose, causing suffocation. This lasts for 1d12 Rounds, but can be ended sooner by the casting of *Bless, Dispel Evil, Protection from Evil,* or *Sanctuary.* A character can go without air for a number of rounds equal to twice her Constitution score. (Repeatable)

78. The characters find a single boy's shoe lying on the ground in front of them (see entry 49). (Repeatable)

79. The characters hear the sound of footsteps behind them, but, when they turn, there is no one there. (Repeatable)

80. A loud buzzing sound is heard, revealing that one of the room's windows is covered in flies. Re-roll if there are no windows nearby. (Repeatable)

81. The character with the highest Charisma feels herself being embraced by an invisible entity. (Repeatable)

82. A nearby window opens, allowing a strong wind to blow into the room briefly before stopping. Re-roll if there are no windows nearby. (Repeatable)

83. The area is under a magical effect identical to *Silence, 15' Radius* except that it affects the entire area only for as long as the characters are within it. (Repeatable)

84. The doorknob the characters have just touched is painfully hot to the touch (dealing 1d4 damage). If there is no door nearby, nothing happens. (Repeatable)

85. The next time one of the characters speaks, she hears a disembodied voice say, "Shhhh!" (Repeatable)

86. The characters hear the hiss of a cat. (Repeatable)

87. The area is covered in spiderwebs. The webs are non-magical in nature and can easily be removed with some effort, but they are everywhere. (Repeatable)

88. After the characters enter the next area, they hear a knocking at the door through which they just came. No one is there. If no doors are nearby, nothing happens. (Repeatable)

89. A figure in a portrait, tapestry, mural, or other piece of nearby artwork noticeably moves. (Repeatable)

90. The character with the highest Wisdom feels as if someone has just laid a hand on her shoulder. (Repeatable)

91. An unpleasant, rotten odor suffuses the area. (Repeatable)

92. The characters hear the sound of clanking chains. (Repeatable)

93. The highest level spellcaster (choose Cleric over Magic-User) feels warm breath on the back of her neck. If there are no spellcasters in the party, re-roll. (Repeatable)

94. Bloody footprints appear on the ground and fade as soon as they are touched by the characters. (Repeatable)

95. The crying of a small child can be heard. (Repeatable)

96. The characters hear the baying of a dog or wolf. (Repeatable)

97. A large (but not unnaturally so) rat scurries across the ground and into a hole. (Repeatable)

98. A table (or similar piece of furniture) in the next area holds a plate of recently cooked meat. The meat is of unknown provenance and tastes a little peculiar but is perfectly fine to eat. (Repeatable)

99. Greenish slime drips from the ceiling onto the floor. The slime is harmless and leaves no permanent stains on either the ceiling or the floor. If outdoors, nothing happens. (Repeatable)

100. A nearby painting falls off the wall. Re-roll if outdoors. (Repeatable)

the barrier

HE MOST IMMEDIATE effect of the chateau's curse is the magical barrier that encloses it. The barrier is a three-dimensional cube that covers the entirety of the chateau and its grounds. The barrier is semi-permeable, allowing free entrance through it into the chateau's grounds, but preventing all egress (by any means, whether physical or magical) until the curse is lifted (see p.26). This means that it neutralizes the functioning of any spell that would enable movement beyond the barrier (though Joudain enjoys seeing the characters attempt to cast them, see p.27). Using these guidelines, the Referee is the final arbiter of what spells are thus prohibited from use. Attempting to cast any non-functional spells removes the spell from the character's memory, just as if she had successfully cast it. In addition, each such attempt merits a roll on the Random Events table (see p.8).

Once on the chateau's grounds beyond the maze, characters are free to move about as they wish. This means that they may travel inside and outside the chateau without any difficulty. The only movement that is completely prohibited is movement outside the barrier. Characters attempting to do so by, for example, climbing over the wall surrounding the grounds or walking out of the hedge maze will discover a hard but invisible wall of magical energy. Touching this wall does no harm to the character, but hitting it with any ordinary implement, including weapons, results in the item being shattered (and a roll on the Random Events table).

the household staff

URING HIS LIFETIME, Lord Joudain employed a large number of servants, some of whom lived on the grounds of the chateau itself. Many of those servants can still be found here, albeit no longer alive in the usual sense. Each is now a unique type of undead creature, the descriptions of which follow overleaf (see p.16 to 23).

using the household staff

ANY OF THE CHATEAU'S staff can only be encountered as a result of random rolls on the Random Event table. Consequently, it is important that the Referee familiarize himself with the descriptions above in order to use these unique undead beings to their fullest when the dice indicate their appearance. Most of the chateau's keyed areas are devoid of permanent inhabitants. Indeed, many of them are largely empty of anything of real interest, which is why the household staff play such a vital role in keeping the adventure compelling.

To varying degrees, the household staff all labor under the effects of the curse that binds Joudain's consciousness to the chateau. This has not only preserved them in their undead state, it has also twisted their minds and reduced most of them to insanity. Unless their descriptions say otherwise, every time they are encountered, the Referee should roll on the Reaction table found in the Rules & Magic book to determine how they will react to the presence of the Player Characters—every time.

The unpredictability of the household staff is important, since it contributes to the lack of safety the Player Characters ought to feel while inside the chateau. With few exceptions, there is no way of determining that a servant you met earlier will react the same way the next time you encounter him or her. Some players may find this frustrating, and they should. The chateau is a frustrating, maddening place, especially in the beginning, before they have had a chance to explore it and gain some inkling of what is going on and how they might manipulate the situation to their advantage. Until then, they should feel they have been thrown headlong into a sinister, chaotic fun house.

a note about language

The inhabitants of the province of Averenha speak Occitan, a Romance language related to French but distinct from it. Therefore, the household staff of the chateau also speak Occitan. The usual LotFP language rules apply when attempting to understand or communicate with these undead beings. Characters who already know French or Italian gain a +1 bonus when trying to make sense of Occitan. Throughout this adventure, assume that any written or spoken language is Occitan, unless otherwise specified. Spells that enable the caster to speak with the dead or to communicate wordlessly with another creature work on the household staff, however, despite what the standard descriptions of those spells might say.

ARNAUD - Land Steward

> **ARNAUD: Armor 12, Move 60', 2 Hit Dice, 12hp, punch 1d8, Morale 12.**

In life, Arnaud was responsible for managing Lord Joudain's properties outside the walls of his chateau. He also collected the rents from peasant farmers who lived on Joudain's lands and made use of his fields. This position was extremely prestigious and he considered himself a gentleman of means rather than a mere household servant. Consequently, he was not well liked by most of the other members of Joudain's staff, especially the maids and footmen, who considered him snobbish and aloof. Lord Joudain himself was not overly fond of him either, but continued to retain his services because he was very good at his job and devoted all of his time to it. Eventually, though, Arnaud spoke ill of Ysabel in Joudain's presence and that was enough to sign his death warrant. Joudain slew him with his sword and reanimated him later, but sewed his lips shut so that he might never again utter a word against Ysabel. Even in undeath, his lips remain sewn.

BERTRAND - Groom

> **BERTRAND: Armor 12, Move 90', 1 Hit Die, 6hp, 1 claw 1d6, Morale 12.**

Bertrand was fourteen when he entered Joudain's service. He was the son of tenants who hoped that he might make a better life for himself by working in the lord's service. Their hopes were somewhat misplaced, as Bertrand was a layabout and a shirker, which did little to endear him to anyone, least of all Martin the stable master.

His lackadaisical attitude toward his work eventually resulted in his not having Joudain's preferred riding horse (named Jakelin) available in time for an important journey he was about to undertake. In retribution, the master branded him with a hot iron until he died from the pain and shock. He still bears the scars of that torture even in death.

CLARETA - Chamber Maid

> **CLARETA:** Armor 17, Move 150', 4 Hit Dice, 26hp, 1 touch 1d8, Morale 12. Each time a touch deals 6 or more points of damage, the target must make a saving throw versus Magic or lose experience points down to halfway up the previous level. Clareta is incorporeal.

Clareta had been in the service of the Ayarai family for decades. Joudain remembered her fondly from his childhood, when she would often sneak him sweets from the kitchen, despite the disapproval of his guardians and teachers. She doted on him, praising his good looks and fine intelligence, feeding Joudain's ego and encouraging him to believe that he could get anything he wanted, because he was, after all, the Master of the chateau.

When Clareta died at an advanced age, Joudain deeply missed her. One of the few times he can remember actually praying to God was when he asked that Clareta be restored to life like Lazarus of Bethany in the Gospel of St. John. When this did not happen as he demanded, it only confirmed to him that God was, at best, a myth or, at worst, impotent. Regardless, he had no need for belief in him. When Joudain committed suicide and his consciousness was bound to the chateau, he found he could call Clareta's ghost from beyond the grave and she has served here ever since.

ELIAS - House Steward

> **ELIAS:** Armor 12, Move 60', 3 Hit Dice, 18hp, 1 strike 1d8, Morale 12. Elias can absorb up to 8 spell levels cast within 10' of him, negating their effects. Each time he absorbs spell energy in this way, his head grows noticeably larger. After reaching 8 total spell levels, his head explodes, dealing 2d6 damage to all within 10'. If this occurs, Elias is irrevocably destroyed and not even Joudain can restore him to un-life.

Elias was responsible for all household purchasing, as well as for hiring, firing, and paying the staff. Though not as lofty a position as that of land steward, it was nevertheless important and Elias took pride in it. He also possessed an extraordinary memory, making him very good at his job. Elias had a longstanding rivalry with Arnaud (see p.16)—a rivalry that Joudain subtly encouraged by telling each of his servants about the latest slight or unkind word the other had spoken. Most often this resulted merely in arguments, but occasionally it would lead to fistfights.

Elias was very loyal to Joudain and remained in his service until he died of fever. Consequently, he was one of the first servants whom Joudain reanimated. Unfortunately, the effects of the fever—paralysis—remained even after death and Elias moves somewhat slowly and stiffly. In addition, his face is grotesquely contorted by rigor, which impairs his ability to speak clearly.

ESTÈVE - Valet

GUILHÈM - Page

ESTÈVE: Armor 14, Move 90', 2 Hit Dice, 14hp, two claws 1d4 damage each, Morale 12. Anyone struck by Estève must save versus Paralyzation or be paralyzed for 3d6 Turns.

GUILHÈM: Armor 15, Move 120', 1 Hit Die, 5hp, 1 punch 1d4, Morale 12. Guilhèm is incorporeal.

Estève was Joudain's valet, responsible for dressing him, laundering his clothes, and accompanying him on journeys outside the chateau. Unsurprisingly, he developed a high opinion of himself and lorded it over other members of the staff, especially Laurensa (see p.21) and Rixenda (see p.22), from whom he often demanded sexual favors in exchange for the additional monetary compensation he received from the Master as he undertook his duties.

In life, Estève was a strong, stocky man with a hearty appetite. Lord Joudain took advantage of this by ensuring that he partook of Hervisse's "special" meals (see p.19), which ultimately resulted in his current state. He is now a ravenous nigh-immortal mockery of his former self.

Guilhèm was an orphaned peasant boy who came to the chateau begging for food. Though Elias (see p.17) initially sought to turn him away, Joudain thought otherwise, seeing in the boy an opportunity to mold the child's mind in his own image. The Master "adopted" the boy and intended to corrupt him by initiating him into all his depraved activities. However, Joudain never did so for reasons he was never able to explain, and he instead protected and cared for Guilhèm, shielding him from the evil that was going on in the chateau to the best of his abilities.

Guilhèm died when he was ten years old after a fall from the window of the Observatory (see p66). Joudain sincerely mourned his death and continued to ponder why it was that he had such affection for the boy. After Joudain committed suicide, he found that Guilhèm's consciousness lingered about the chateau as well.

HERVISSE - Chef

> **HERVISSE:** Armor 12, Move 60',
> 2 Hit Dice, 13hp, 1 cleaver 1d8,
> Morale 12.

Hervisse was Joudain's chef and a close collaborator with his master. A cruel, jealous man, Hervisse killed a fellow servant whom he had caught spying on Mondette (see p.22) while she bathed. He then chopped up the servant's body and fed it to the Master's dogs. Joudain discovered this, but rather than being angry, he lauded Hervisse for his actions and asked if his chef would be willing to make meals of human meat if he provided it for him. Hervisse readily agreed.

Hervisse was a tall, skinny man in life. He and his wife, Mondette, regularly argued with one another, but he loved her in an angry, possessive way. He never consumed any of the cannibalistic meals he prepared. His consciousness was called back from the Beyond by Joudain.

JAUME & MIQÈL - 1st & 2nd Footmen

> **JAUME & MIQÈL:** Armor 14, Move 90',
> 3 Hit Dice, 19hp (Jaume), 15hp (Miqèl),
> 1 punch 1d8, Morale 12.

Jaume was tall, handsome, and charming—qualities that made him perfect for his duties as a footman, which consisted of greeting guests, opening doors, and serving meals, as well as occasionally accompanying Lord Joudain on his journeys outside the chateau. In these duties, he was assisted by his younger twin brother Miqèl.

Jaume made the most unfortunate mistake of seducing Ysabel (see p.23) and taking her virginity, a sacrilege for which the sentence was death. Enraged upon finding this out, Joudain cleaved Jaume's head in two with an axe and then raised him from the dead to continue his duties. Not long afterward, Joudain decided that, because the twin footmen no longer "matched," he had no choice but to inflict the same fate on Miqèl, who now looks exactly like his older brother.

JULIAN - Gardener

LANDRI - Majordomo

JULIAN: Armor 13, Move 60', 2 Hit Dice, 12hp, 1 bite 1d4, Morale 12. Bite causes rotting disease unless treated with holy water; disease permanently removes 1 point of Constitution per week. Julian is incorporeal.

Julian maintained the gardens outside the chateau, which seemed to be his only true interest. Indeed, Julian seemed to take little notice of much of anything else, preferring to spend his time outside (even at night), working in the dirt and mud in order to ensure that the Master's home was as beautiful as possible. For that reason, he lacked social niceties or concern for his own appearance, much to the chagrin of the other servants, who were always cleaning up after him when he entered the chateau.

In life, Julian was a small, balding man of advanced years. When he died, he was buried in the garden, under his beloved rose bushes (area M13, see p.36). Joudain called to his consciousness after he committed suicide and his incorporeal form answered.

LANDRI: Armor 12, Move 60', 3 Hit Dice, 17hp, 1 punch 1d4, Morale 12.

Landri was the highest ranking of Lord Joudain's servants proper. He kept the other servants working according to their schedules and ensured that things ran smoothly so as not to elicit the ire of the Master. He was very good at his job and well compensated for it, but he was never comfortable with his employment. Unlike most of the staff, Landri was a devout believer who attended Mass daily and prayed intently for the conversion of Lord Joudain's heart.

Joudain kept Landri around, because it amused him to taunt and mock him and his beliefs. He even hoped that he might eventually break him, but it never occurred and Landri remained steadfast in his faith. Annoyed by this, Joudain slew Landri with his sword in the Chapel (see p.48) and then raised him from the dead in that very room, using it to once more sneer at Landri's faith. The majordomo still bears the wounds from his death on his body. As majordomo, he carries with him a large key that enables him to open the doors to most rooms of the chateau.

LAURENSA - Parlor Maid

MARTIN - Stable Master

LAURENSA: Armor 14, Move 90', 2 Hit Dice, 11hp, two claw attacks 1d4 damage each, Morale 12. Anyone struck by Laurensa must save versus Paralyzation or be paralyzed for 3d6 Turns.

MARTIN: Armor 16, Move 60', 3 Hit Dice, 20hp, 42 claw attacks 1d8 each, Morale 12.

Laurensa was a parlor maid, which meant that she was responsible for cleaning the various "outer" rooms of the chateau (i.e. not living quarters, like bedrooms, etc.). This made her one of the lowest ranking members of the staff's internal hierarchy, though this did not bother her. Laurensa was a pretty but vapid peasant girl who was simply happy to be employed in such a grand home. She was easily persuaded to do what others asked of her, especially Estève (see p.18), who frequently took advantage of her naïveté.

Like the valet, Laurensa has become a bestial mockery of her former self. Her hair is a wild mess and her once-attractive features are now contorted with a lust for human flesh, which she consumes in order to maintain her existence.

An unpleasant man who loved horses more than he loved people, Martin enjoyed bullying Bertrand (see p.16) and, for that matter, anyone else who got in his way. He was disliked by the rest of the chateau staff and so rarely entered its halls. Instead, he preferred to rule over his little domain and curry favor with Lord Joudain by doing special errands for him, such as kidnapping peasants for use in his various experiments.

While alive, Martin was a large, strong-limbed man with a beard and mustache. He was missing one eye, which he had lost during his time as a soldier, but he did not wear an eyepatch or other covering, preferring to leave the empty socket visible for all to see. This no doubt contributed to the dislike the rest of the staff had for him.

MONDETTE - Kitchen Maid

RIXENDA - Chamber Maid

**MONDETTE: Armor 14, Move 90',
2 Hit Dice, 13hp, 2 claws 1d6 damage
each, Morale 12.**

Mondette was the wife of Hervisse
(see p.19), with whom she had a
tempestuous relationship. She frequently
berated and belittled him, in addition to
behaving in a coquettish fashion while in
the presence of other men. She enjoyed
arousing her husband's anger and often
used it as a way to exact her revenge
on others. More than once, she feigned
interest in another servant, only to have
Hervisse beat (and, in one case, kill) him,
much to her delight.

Mondette eventually pushed her
husband too far and he killed her in
a rage, planting a cleaver in the back
of her head. Though now reanimated,
she still bears the marks of that wound.

**RIXENDA: Armor 14, Move 90', 2 Hit
Dice, 13hp, two claws 1d4 damage
each, Morale 12.** Anyone struck by
Rixenda must save versus Paralyzation
or be paralyzed for 3d6 Turns.

Older and plainer than Laurensa
(see p.21), Rixenda was the chateau's
chamber maid and thus had access to
the bedrooms of the chateau. She had
come to Joudain's service after fleeing
an abusive marriage and her body bore
scars from the beatings she received at
the hands of her husband. Her husband
once came to the chateau looking for
her and the Master had Martin beat
him to death so that he would never
harm her again, thereby earning her
undying loyalty.

Rixenda now bears only passing
resemblance to her living self. She
is wild-eyed and bestial and survives
on a diet of flesh, preferably that of
human beings.

YSABEL - Maid

YSABEL: Armor 12, Move 90', 5 Hit Dice, 29hp, 1 touch 1d8, Morale 12. Her weeping requires saving throw versus Magic by all within 10 feet of her. Those who fail suffer a random effect (1d6) for the next 5 Rounds: 1. Attack Ysabel; 2. No effect; 3–4. Uncontrollable weeping; 5. Wanders away; 6. Attacks allies. Ysabel is incorporeal.

In his blasphemous Black Masses, Joudain needed a young and virginal woman whose naked body would serve as his altar. He found such a woman in Ysabel, whom he brought to the chateau after searching across southern France for a "perfect" woman with all the right qualities he sought. Though ostensibly a maid, Joudain treated her very well and provided for her every need, provided she never leave his domain and that she perform her "religious" duties without complaint.

In time, Jaume (see p.19) seduced Ysabel and her deflowering made her no longer suitable for Joudain's purposes. He killed Jaume in retaliation and Ysabel, her sanity already tenuous by this point, took her own life by drinking poison. He tried to reanimate her like his other servants but, for some reason, the process did not work as he had hoped and the result was a semi-corporeal ghost-like being with transparent "skin" who spends most of her undead existence weeping.

undead immunities and resistances

Broadly speaking, all of the household staff are undead creatures. As such, they share certain traits in common, regardless of their other unique abilities. All of the staff can see 60 feet in the dark. They are immune to all mind-affecting spells (charms, illusions, etc.), as well as poison, *Sleep*, paralysis, stunning, and disease. Finally, they make no noise unless the text specifies that they do so.

Corporeal undead are immune to the "lower half" of all weapon damage dice rolled against them. For example, a medium weapon deals 1d8 damage. When used against a corporeal undead, only rolls of 5–8 deal any damage. Spells deal normal damage, however.

Incorporeal undead are immune to all physical attacks; they can only be harmed by spells or other magical effects.

turning undead

 IVEN THE NATURE OF THE chateau, it might come as a surprise that the 1st-level Clerical spell *Turn Undead* works just fine within its walls. The spell can be used largely as described in the Rules & Magic book. Joudain's curse may keep his household staff active long after their deaths, but it is not so strong that it can wholly circumvent the divine power inherent in this spell.

That said, there are a couple of small caveats. Firstly, all incorporeal undead who are successfully turned flee by vanishing from sight. They simply disappear and are not seen again unless and until the characters encounter them again, either by entering an area whose description includes them or as a result of a Random Event roll.

Corporeal undead literally flee from the sight of the Cleric and her holy symbol, moving as quickly as possible to a place of safety. In such a case, the Referee must determine a suitably "safe" location and remember that the undead servant can now be found there.

In the event of a "D" result, the servant is destroyed and thus cannot be encountered by any means for the next 24 hours. On the next day, the servant is "reborn" and can be encountered once more. However, from that point on, do not make a Reaction roll for the servant in question. Instead, she is implacably Hostile toward the Player Characters and will do everything within her power to attack or otherwise impede them while they remain within the chateau.

energy drain

HE GHOSTLY TOUCH OF Dame Helissente (in location U6, p.65) causes "energy drain." This is a powerful destruction of life essence that is thoroughly devastating to its victim. Here are several possible effects it has on a victim; choose one or roll randomly each time the power is employed. The effects of energy drain are permanent and cannot normally be reversed:

d6	ENERGY DRAIN EFFECT
1.	The victim loses one level's worth of hit points.
2.	The victim loses enough experience points to lose a level. The new experience point total is set at the mid-point of the new level. Any and all benefits of the previous level (hit points, attack bonus, saving throw increases, etc.) are lost until enough experience points are earned to regain the lost level.
3.	The victim loses 1d4 points of Constitution.
4.	The victim is drained not of physical vitality but of will. She suffers a -1 penalty to hit, damage, and initiative rolls.
5.	The victim loses youth. Each energy drain ages her 1d10 years.
6.	Reroll, with Dame Helissente gaining the abilities lost by the victim. If the victim loses hit points, Helissente gains them. If the victim loses a level, Helissente gains a Hit Die, etc. If the victim is aged, Helissente gains 1 Hit Die per attack that ages a victim.

If the victim is drained to 0 level, 0 hit points, or 0 Constitution from energy drain, she dies.

dying within the chateau

CONSEQUENCE OF the curse is that the consciousness of anyone who dies on the grounds of the chateau is trapped here forever—unless the curse is lifted. This has two effects. First, in the unlikely event that the Player Characters (or anyone else) possess some means to restore the dead to life (such as a magic item), that restoration will be incomplete. The formerly-dead individual is now "alive" in the sense that her body becomes active once again. She may walk, talk, fight, and generally engage in any other physical activity. However, her Charisma and Wisdom scores are reduced to 3. She can no longer cast spells, be affected by any beneficial Clerical magic, or gain experience. In all other respects, the character is the same as before her demise.

Second—and more importantly—a character who dies on the chateau's grounds can be reanimated by Joudain as the result of certain results on the Random Event table. Such characters become NPCs under the control of the Referee and are governed by the same general rules as the household staff (see Using the Household Staff, p.15). At the Referee's discretion, reanimated Player Characters may provide some assistance to their former comrades if the results on the reaction table are "Talkative" or "Helpful." Such assistance is limited, of course, as they will know comparatively little about the chateau or Lord Joudain. Regardless, it is important that the Referee treat them as undead creatures, not as the human beings they once were. They are now thralls of Joudain and behave accordingly.

escaping the chateau

S NOTED PREVIOUSLY, Lord Joudain traps anyone who enters the grounds of his chateau in the hope that they might entertain him sufficiently to free him from his ennui and thus sever the spiritual link to his former home. Thus far, he has only limited evidence that this is even possible, since all of the previous "visitors" to the chateau have died before he could fully put his theory to the test, but he continues to try nevertheless. Fortunately for the characters, Lord Joudain is in fact correct. Unfortunately for them, freeing his consciousness requires that those trapped not merely suffer misfortune at his hands but that they survive long enough to suffer enough misfortune to divert him and thereby lift the curse.

To do that, the Referee should keep track of Joudain's Fun, as the characters explore the chateau. Joudain's Fun starts at 0 and increases according to the table opposite. The list is not exhaustive by any means. The Referee should add his own conditions to the list, using those here as a guideline. In general, positive or beneficial actions bore Lord Joudain and thus lower the running tally of Joudain's Fun, while negative or harmful actions entertain him and thus increase it. The points lost for positive actions should (again, in general) be greater than those gained for negative actions. That is because Joudain, after decades of entrapment, is not easily entertained, making it much easier to frustrate his efforts at diversion than to satiate them. Joudain's Fun cannot go below 0.

If, through the Player Characters' actions Joudain's Fun reaches 100, they will then hear a disembodied voice shout out, "The curse is lifted! I am free!" The chateau continues as it did before except that the Referee no longer rolls on the Random Events table (see p.8). Likewise, any creatures created through the agency of Lord Joudain (such as the household staff) collapse immediately into dust.

Its master now free to move on from this earthly plane, the chateau could in theory be claimed by the Player Characters (or anyone else) as their own. In addition, the magical barrier preventing escape is now lifted and the characters may leave the chateau grounds if they choose to do so. Of course, local authorities, the Church, distant scions of the Ayarai family, and so on, might have other ideas...

joudain's fun

- +1 per 2 points of damage suffered by any Player Character (cumulative)
- +1 per keyed area explored in the chateau or its grounds
- +1 per combat in which the party engages
- +1 per failed saving throw by a Player Character
- +1 per prohibited spell a Player Character attempts to cast (see Front Gate, p.40)
- +1 per attempt to break through the magical barrier with any implement
- +1 per member of the household staff encountered
- +1 per time a Player Character utters a curse (+2 if she curses God, the saints, etc.)
- +1 per time a Player Character verbally expresses fear ("I'm frightened," "This is scary," etc.)
- +2 per ability point lost/drained by any means
- +2 per failed attempt to use *Turn Undead* on one of the household staff
- +5 if the Player Characters present Ysabel with lilacs (see p.36)
- +5 if the Player Characters destroy Arnaud or Jaume
- +5 per new token left at the grave of Ysabel at area M12 (see p.36)
- +10 per act of kindness shown toward Guilhèm or Ysabel
- +10 per level drained
- +20 per Player Character death
- -1 per 1 point of damage healed
- -2 per successful saving throw by a Player Character
- -2 per time a Player Character exhorts her companions to be brave
- -3 per ability point gained/restored by any means
- -3 per time a Player Character praises God, the saints, etc.
- -4 per successful use of *Turn Undead* on one of the household staff
- -5 per attempt to break through a hedge maze wall
- -10 per token taken from the grave of Ysabel at area M12 (see p.36)
- -10 if the bones of Ysabel at area M12 (see p.36) are in any way disturbed
- -15 per level restored by any means
- -20 if the characters destroy Guilhèm or Ysabel
- -25 per character restored to life by any means

the chateau

map key

HE CHATEAU GROUNDS are divided into several sections, each of which is identified with a different letter. These sections are: the hedge maze (M), the chateau grounds (C), the ground level (G) and upper level (U) of the chateau, and its basement (B).

LIGHTING

Unless otherwise noted in an area's description, the chateau is unlit. Most rooms can be assumed to have wall sconces for candles and some even have candelabra or chandeliers. Unless lit by the Player Characters (or because of results on the Random Event table), however, they shed no light whatsoever. It is also worth noting that the usual day/night cycle continues to occur even after Joudain has erected the magical barrier over the chateau's grounds. Therefore the Referee should note the time when the Player Characters arrive, and keep track of the passage of time so to tailor his descriptions of the chateau's rooms accordingly.

PAINTINGS

The predominant form of decoration in the chateau is the framed painting, the majority of which are portraits. Unless otherwise noted, most rooms contain 1d6 paintings on their walls.

The Referee is free to describe these paintings however he wishes or he can make use of the following random table for inspiration:

d20	PAINTING
1	Still life
2	Nature painting
3	Fantastical, distorted painting of nature
4	Portrait of a young woman
5	Portrait of a man and a woman
6	Painting depicting a mythological scene
7	Painting depicting a religious scene
8	Portrait of a child
9	Portrait of an old man
10	Portrait of a man or woman dressed in royal finery
11	Landscape
12	Fantastical, distorted landscape
13	An equestrian portrait
14	A female nude
15	An anatomical painting
16	A painting of a monster
17	The Dance of Death or another macabre scene
18	A battle scene
19	Ships at sea
20	An obviously foreign painting (e.g. Chinese, Arabian, etc.)

If removed from the chateau and sold, each painting is worth 1d10x10sp (re-roll and add if result of "100" is achieved).

OTHER ROOM CONTENTS

The chateau has been abandoned for decades prior to the arrival of the Player Characters. In the ensuing decades, the effects of the curse have largely preserved the chateau from ordinary decay, meaning that the place still largely looks like it did during Lord Joudain's lifetime. However, dust still accumulates in the place, spiders still spin webs, and other vermin, like rats, still cause damage. In addition, other travelers arrived here before the characters, and their activities may have wrought some havoc. Any damage caused by visitors to the chateau is generally not repaired by the curse's effects, meaning that if, for example, the Player Characters break a chair or set fire to some tapestries the damage they do will remain.

Consequently, the room descriptions that follow assume that many rooms are "empty" in that they have few furnishings or noteworthy features. This is intentional. First, it is intended to reflect the deleterious effects of the passage of time, including the exploration of previous travelers. Second, and more importantly, it is because, upon the Player Characters' entering any room, the Referee rolls on the Random Event table to determine what awaits them. In most cases, the result of that roll will provide enough mystery, interest, and/or danger to hold their attention.

Of course, the Referee should feel free to add more contents to any room, if he feels it will make for a better adventure.

hedge maze

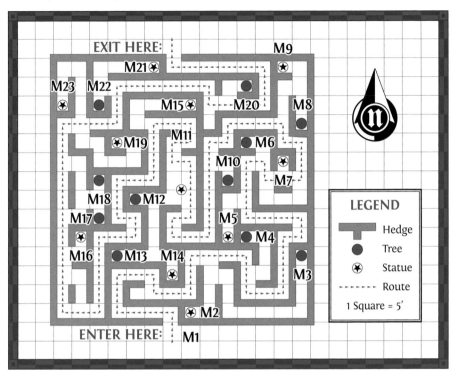

LEGEND

⊤	Hedge
●	Tree
✪	Statue
------►	Route
1 Square = 5′	

EXIT HERE: • M9 • M21✪ • M23 • M22 • M15✪ • M20 • M8 • M11 • M19✪ • M6 • M10 • M7 • M18 • M12 • M17 • M5 • M4 • M16 • M13 • M14 • M3 • M2✪ • ENTER HERE: M1

N FRONT OF THE CHATEAU proper is a large hedge maze. Its current location is a result of the curse. Originally, the maze was located behind the chateau, south of the stable (C5) and kennel (C6), but still within the walls surrounding the grounds. Once the curse took effect, Joudain used his new-found abilities to move the maze from behind the chateau and placed it and all that it contained in front of area C1. Characters who look at the grounds will see parts of the grass and earth have been upturned, as if something large and heavy had been dragged from behind the chateau to in front of it.

Consequently, the maze is now the only way to reach the chateau grounds (see p.40). Though it is presently far from its original location, the magical barrier the curse generates (see p.14) affects the maze as well. However, any character who travels above the top of the maze by any means and then descends below it again is stuck by a lightning bolt dealing 3d6 damage (save versus Magic for half-damage). The thorny shrubs that make up the maze stand eight feet tall. Their leaves and branches are thick enough that it is impossible to see through them to the other side. The shrubs are always well manicured by Julian (see p.20).

M1. MAZE ENTRANCE

A wooden archway, emblazoned with the single word "Ayarai," marks the entrance to the hedge maze. Once a character passes beyond this archway, she cannot leave the maze again, as the magical barrier described above prevents it. The only option is to move forward.

M2. STATUE OF SAVIÉ AYARAI

A stone statue stands upon a plinth that identifies it as depicting Savié Ayarai. The sculpting of the statue is fairly crude and shows obvious signs of weathering. Savié is depicted as a knight, wearing armor and with his shield (bearing the Ayarai family crest) at his feet.

M3. LILAC BUSH

Regardless of the time of year or weather, a lilac bush flourishes here. The bush smells quite fragrant. Anyone who leans in to smell its flowers must make a saving throw versus Breath Weapon or collapse into a deep sleep from which she can only awaken after 1d4 Turns. While asleep, the character dreams of a beautiful woman admiring the lilacs in the company of an older gentleman. The woman is Ysabel (see p.23) and the gentleman is Lord Joudain. Should a character take a clipping of the flowers and later present them to Ysabel, there is a bonus to Joudain's Fun (see p.27).

M4. PEAR TREE

Growing here is a small pear tree. The tree is planted upon the place where Lord Joudain buried the body of his one-time lover, Catarina de Margelasse, the daughter of a provincial gentleman. He murdered her, because she accused him—correctly, it should be mentioned—of having other lovers. Joudain never bothered to reanimate her after death and so her remains are still here. However, the curse has affected the tree—or rather its fruit, all of which are red in color and bear the name of Catarina on their skins, as if written in ink. Eating one of these pears has no adverse effects whatsoever.

M5. STATUE OF SILVAN AYARAI

The stone statue in this alcove depicts Silvan Ayarai, as identified by a plaque near its feet. Silvan is dressed in an older style of clothing, from at least a century prior to the present. He is shown holding an open book in one hand. Carved upon the open pages of the book is the Latin verse "Melius est dies mortis quam die nativitatis," which is an allusion to Ecclesiastes 7:2, where it is stated that "better is the day of death than the day of one's birth."

M6. SHRIVELED BUSH

A dry and bare bush stands here. There are no leaves on its branches nor on the ground surrounding it, suggesting that it has been dead for quite some time.

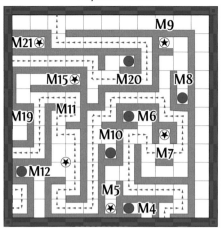

1 square = 5 feet

M7. STATUE OF FELISE AYARAI

A bronze statue of an older woman occupies this area of the maze. The statue is disturbingly lifelike and a character who stares at it for more than a Round must make a saving throw versus Magic. A character who fails will believe she sees the statue pivot on its plinth and is overcome with fear of it. Consequently, she will flee from it and cannot bring herself to come closer than 10 feet to it. This effect is permanent; only magical effects can force the character to ever approach the statue without trepidation. Felise holds in her hands two goblets. Any liquid placed in the goblet in her left hand cures the drinker of any diseases or neutralizes any poison in her system. Any liquid placed in the goblet in her right hand heals the drinker for 1d6+1 hit points. Each character can use the goblets a number of times equal to her Charisma modifier. Any subsequent attempts seem to work but instead create a deadly poison. Liquid transformed by the goblets retains its potency even if bottled and taken elsewhere.

M8. FACES

The bush in this area is covered with brilliant red flowers very similar in general appearance to daisies. However, in place of the central disc, these flowers instead have mockeries of human faces—two eyes, a nose, and a mouth. These faces take notice of anyone who approaches them by grimacing in obvious disgust. The flowers also make quiet mewling noises, as if they were talking to one another. However, these noises do not constitute any sort of communication. Therefore, even magic does not make them intelligible to the characters. If touched, the flowers attempt to bite (dealing 1 point of damage per hit). If a flower is cut from the bush, it immediately withers and dies; its petals turn gray and the face in the center closes its eyes and mouth.

M9. STATUE OF JAUFRE AYARAI

The bronze statue of a regal-looking man stands here. His head, which reaches above the top of the hedge maze, wears a coronet that indicates his status as a baron. The statue's face looks down upon anyone who views it with imperious contempt.

M10. XAVIER D'ESPIVANT

The earth in this alcove looks fresh and recently turned. There is a small green bush planted here, but sticking up from the earth beneath it are the feet and fingers of a human being. The flesh of these extremities is pale and desiccated. If anyone attempts to dig up the body buried beneath the bush, she will find that it is a naked man out of whose crushed chest the roots of the bush grow. Of course, doing so summons Julian (see p.20) in 1d10 Rounds, who first warns the characters, "The Master would not be pleased with what you are doing. Stop at once or face his wrath." If the characters do not immediately cease digging up the dirt beneath the bush, Julian audibly sighs and attacks the characters. He will keep up his attack until he is destroyed, the characters are all slain, or the characters flee the area. Julian will then begin to cover up the body again and will not depart the area until the job is done.

The body beneath the bush is that of Xavier d'Espivant, a wealthy traveler from Las Chòtas, a village in the southern part of Averenha. Xavier had the misfortune to come upon the chateau and enter it, during which time Lord Joudain found him insufficiently entertaining and allowed Miqèl and Jaume (see p.19) to slay him. Spells that grant the ability to communicate with the dead work on Xavier, who died less than one year ago. He knows little of the history of the chateau or its inhabitants, but he does remember a fair bit about the layout of the grounds and the chateau itself. He also knows that Lord Joudain prizes diversion above all else and expresses regret that he was unable to amuse the master of the chateau and thereby remain among the living.

M11. STATUE OF JOUDAIN AYARAI

A large bronze statue of Lord Joudain as an adult (see G17, p52) towers above this open area. Joudain's face has an extremely bored expression upon it. The statue also depicts human bones, weapons, and implements of torture lying at Joudain's feet. A character who looks at the statue must make a successful saving throw versus Magic or be overcome with ennui and despair, suffering a -2 penalty to attack and damage rolls and saving throws for the next 1d8 Turns. However, any character who fails the saving throw also hears a voice inside her head, asking, "Is there nothing that can relieve my boredom?"

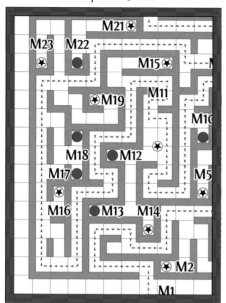

appear if the character only picks up a token to look at it and then returns it to its original location; it is only outright theft that summons them. If more than one token is taken away, an additional member of the household staff is summoned, in the following order: Julian (see p.19), Estève (see p.18), Martin (see p.21), one for each token beyond the first. If all the household staff summoned are defeated, Joudain sends no more and the characters are free to take the tokens away with them. However, doing so incurs penalties to Joudain's Fun, as noted on p.27.

As noted above, Ysabel's body lies beneath the lilac bush, consisting only of bones now. Digging them up or otherwise disturbing them also displeases Joudain (see p.27), but he does not summon any members of the household staff to stop this desecration. Spells that grant the ability to communicate with the dead work on Ysabel, but she has been dead for decades now. Ysabel has intimate knowledge of the chateau and its inhabitants, including Lord Joudain.

M12. LILAC BUSH

Another lilac bush, its blossoms more vibrant than those on the bush in area M3 (see p.36) grows here. Beneath this bush lie the remains of Ysabel (see p.23), buried here after her suicide and regularly tended to by Julian (see p.20). This area is immaculately maintained, without so much as a blade of grass or a pebble out of place. There is no external evidence that anyone is buried beneath the bush.

However, there are many tokens of affection placed around the base of the lilac bush. They are: a jeweled necklace (worth 1,000sp), a string of pearls (worth 1,500sp), a silver tiara (worth 1,000sp), and a simple gold locket on which is inscribed the name Ysabel (worth 500sp). Should a character remove one of the tokens from the area, Miqèl and Jaume (see p.19) will appear and attack the character with the intent to kill her. The ghastly brothers do not

M13. ROSE BUSH

Buried beneath this red rose bush is the body of Julian (see p.20), though this is not at all apparent from looking at this alcove, which is extremely well maintained. Attempting to dig beneath the bush summons Julian, who attacks the characters with great ferocity (a +2 bonus to his attack rolls). Should the characters use magic that allows them to communicate with the dead, they can contact Julian (who has been dead decades). His knowledge is mostly limited to the hedge maze and the grounds, as he was rarely allowed into the chateau itself.

M14. STATUE OF JÒRGI AYARAI

The stone statue that stands here depicts a frail-looking old man, seated upon an ornate chair. He is bald and points his finger accusingly at the viewer. There is a small plaque at the statue's base that identifies him, but it is partially covered by muddy soil.

M15. HEADLESS STATUE

Made of stone, the statue in this alcove is now headless, its head having been roughly hacked from atop its neck. The missing head is nowhere to be found. The plaque on the statue's plinth has been effaced (by a knife or some other sharp implement) to such an extent that it is utterly illegible.

M16. WOODEN STATUE

A wooden statue of a large, broad-shouldered man lies propped up against the walls of this alcove. There is no sign of a base or a plaque indicating whom the statue represents. The statue radiates magic. If anyone touches the statue, it springs to life and attacks. If defeated, it falls to the ground and becomes inert once more. Even if it is utterly destroyed, the statue will reform over the course of the next 24 hours, after which it becomes active once again.

> **WOODEN STATUE:** Armor 16, Move 30', 5 Hit Dice, 29hp, 2 punches for 1d8 damage each, Morale 12.

M17. APPLE TREE

A small apple tree stands in this alcove. Its fruits may be eaten without any ill effects.

M18. RASPBERRY BUSH

A red raspberry bush occupies this area. Its berries are not currently ripe, but they are nevertheless edible.

M19. STATUE OF PASCAU AYARAI

A bronze statue of an older man dressed in pilgrim's garb stands here. He bears a staff, a cockel hat, and several badges on his robe that indicate the various shrines he has visited. The plaque on the statue's plinth indicates it depicts Pascau Ayarai and, unlike most of the statues in the hedge maze, gives his birth and death dates (1325–1384). If anyone touches the statue, she is immediately teleported to another location within the hedge maze. The Referee should roll 1d20+1 to determine the area to which the character is magically transported, with any result of 19 indicating area M22. A separate roll is made for each character who touches the statue, even if two or more characters touch the statue simultaneously. The effect works no matter how many characters touch the statue or how many times it is touched. The statue radiates magic.

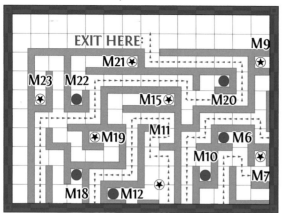

1 square = 5 feet

EXIT HERE

M9
M21 ✪
M23 M22
M15 ✪ ---- M20
M19 M11
M6
M10
M7
M18 M12

Each character can ask a number of questions of the statue equal to her Charisma modifier, after which it will answer no more questions for that character.

M22. CARVED TREE

The tree here was formerly an apple tree, but it is now dead. Its bark has been elaborately carved with grinning skulls and demonic faces.

M20. STRAWBERRY BUSH

This area contains a large and lush strawberry bush, which is covered in large plump berries. While the berries are completely edible, any character who consumes more than one of them finds her skin changes to a brilliant red color. The color change lasts for 1d4 weeks, after which it fades. The change can also be reversed through the casting of any healing or curative spell.

M21. STATUE OF CLOUTILDOU AYARAI

This bronze statue depicts an attractive young woman dressed in the robes of a scholar. There are piles of books and scrolls at her feet. Her arms are open in a welcoming pose. Beneath the plaque that identifies her name is carved the Latin word quæro—"ask." The statue radiates magic. A character who asks any question of the statue hears an answer in her head, delivered in a pleasant, feminine voice. The answer, however, is both incorrect and, where possible, the exact opposite of the truth.

M23. STATUE OF GABRIEÙ AYARAI

This old stone statue depicts a smiling middle-aged man. His arms are out-stretched in an orant position, the palms of his hands facing upwards. Characters who enter this area feel calm and peace-able and do not wish to leave. Such characters must make a successful saving throw versus Paralyzation or be unable to bring themselves to leave for 1d4 Turns. For every Turn a character remains here (whether by choice or because of the magical effects of the statue), she heals 1d6+1 hit points. If a character who fails her saving throw is forced to leave the area against her will before the appropriate number of Turns have elapsed, she instead suffers 2d6+2 damage.

chateau grounds

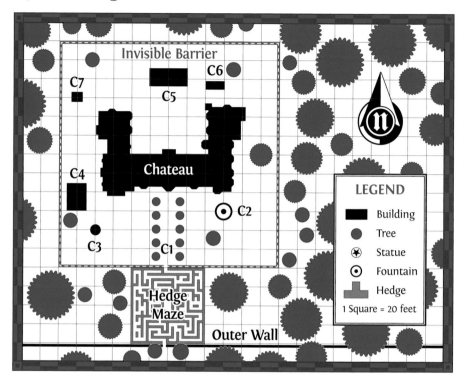

Invisible Barrier
C7
C6
C5
C4
Chateau
C2
C3
C1
Hedge Maze
Outer Wall

LEGEND

■	Building
●	Tree
✹	Statue
⊙	Fountain
⊥	Hedge

1 Square = 20 feet

HE CHATEAU'S GROUNDS consist of the chateau itself and the smaller buildings and areas of interest clustered around it. Each of these areas is described below in its own section.

C1. FRONT GATE

A wrought iron gate bars entrance to the chateau's grounds. The gate squeaks loudly and takes some effort to push open. Once all the Player Characters have passed beyond it, though, it quickly snaps shut and radiates powerful magic to those who can detect it. Neither brute strength nor magic can now breach the gate, which remains securely shut until the conditions specified in

"Escaping the Chateau" (see p.26) are met. A character who passes through the gate cannot return to the hedge maze until the curse is lifted, even if another character remains in the maze and then pushes it open again. This effect does not apply to any member of the household staff, some of whom might be encountered in the hedge maze.

C2. FOUNTAIN

In the courtyard is a circular pool in the center of which is an ornate fountain carved from a bluish stone not native to the province of Averenha. The pool once contained water that has long since dried up, leaving behind only a thin layer of sediment and dead leaves.

The fountain is a three-tiered affair supported by carvings of four hippocampuses. When a character approaches the fountain, it will spring to life, spewing a greenish liquid from the fountain itself and from the mouths of the four hippocampuses. The liquid looks as if it were water thick with algae, but it is not. The liquid is in fact magical in nature, brought into being by Lord Joudain's power, and its effects are different each time someone dares to drink it. Each time someone drinks the liquid—even if it is the same person—roll 1d8 on the following table to determine its effect:

d8 DRINKING FROM THE FOUNTAIN

1-2: No effect. Treat as water in every respect except coloration.

3: The imbiber is healed 1d6+5 hit points.

4: The imbiber shrinks to one inch tall for 1d6 Turns.

5: The imbiber grows to twice her normal size for 1d4 Turns, in the process gaining a +6 Strength modifier and doing +3 damage in mêlée combat.

6: Poison (save versus Poison or die).

7: The imbiber is stiff and unable to move for 1d4 Turns. During this time, she is aware of her surroundings but cannot interact with them in any way. While in this state, the imbiber cannot be harmed.

8+: No obvious effect, but the next three times the Referee is called upon to roll on the Random Event table, he rolls twice, choosing whichever result is an encounter with one of the undead household staff. If neither result is such an encounter, the Referee may simply choose the result he prefers. If, by some chance, both of the results are an encounter, then both occur at the same time—woe to the Player Characters!

The liquid continues to flow from the fountain for as long as the characters are on the grounds of the chateau. Should they stay long enough, the entirety of the pool will fill with the green liquid but will not overflow it. Liquid subsequently taken outside the grounds of the chateau has no effect on its imbiber whatsoever, except tasting like the algae-filled water it appears to be. Liquid taken in bottles or waterskins and imbibed later while on the grounds has a random effect as noted above, but the Referee should add 3 to any result (i.e. a roll of 3 should be read as 6, etc.). The green liquid dries up should the curse be lifted.

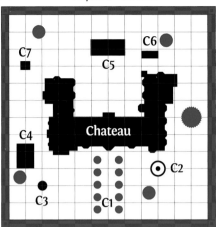

1 square = 20 feet

C3. WELL

There is a stone well located in a corner of the courtyard. The shaft of the well extends close to 40 feet below the chateau's grounds, where it meets an underground freshwater lake. There is in fact nothing of value in the well shaft. Characters who climb down the well in an attempt to escape the magical barrier will find that it leads through many flooded tunnels to the caverns beneath, emerging into the lake in Room B8 of the chateau's underground level (see p.72).

There is a 25% chance that the characters might encounter Julian the gardener (see p.20) here, drawing water from the well with a bucket on a long length of rope. If so, he will be cursing the sorry state of the garden, complaining that no one cares about all the effort he puts into maintaining it. Unless the characters engage him in some way, Julian will ignore them and simply fade away after a few minutes. If someone talks to him, he will eventually gesture toward an empty area of the grounds and complain about how poorly the flowers are doing,

"because no one cares about them—even the Master." There are, of course, no flowers to be seen. If someone questions him or contradicts her about this, he will argue with her and suggest she is "blind" for not being able to see the garden, but will not otherwise escalate the argument. Julian disappears after a few moments, unless he is attacked, in which case he will defend himself.

C4. SMITHY

This small building once housed a smithy used for fashioning metal items used by the inhabitants of the chateau. Lord Joudain also used the smithy in crafting items he would later enchant and, for that reason, he conjured entities of flame to stoke the fires in the forges. The two forges are currently cold and inactive, but if anyone should perform any action within the smithy that generates flame, heat, or light (whether normal or magical), the entities of flame will spring to life once more and attack. The entities attack until either they or their opponents are destroyed. They possess no treasure of their own, but there are two swords in the smithy that, while non-magical, are serviceable enough to use in battle.

> **MINOR ENTITIES OF FLAME: Armor 18, Move 120', 4 Hit Dice, 15hp each, 1 attack for 1d6, Morale 12.** If an entity comes into contact with a flammable substance—by a successful attack against a cloth-wearing opponent or by being struck by a wooden staff, for example—there is a 3 in 6 chance that this attack will spontaneously generate another minor entity of flame that can attack the next Round.

C5. STABLE

This larger building was the chateau's stable, as evinced by a variety of rotting saddles, reins, and other riding gear to be found within. Also to be found are the bones of three horses, each within a stall bearing its name (Galien, Jakelin, and Vuissance, respectively). The bones are just as they appear to be and there is nothing of value here beyond the aforementioned equestrian accoutrements.

Martin (see p.43) is always to be found here, unless he has been destroyed. There is also a 75% chance that Bertrand (see p.16) is here as well. If Martin is alone when encountered, he will discourage the characters from entering, saying that "The stable is full, I'm afraid. Seek out Bertrand and he will find a place to put your horses." If the characters do not do as he says, he will attack them, but only with the purpose of kicking them out of the stable. He has no wish to kill them, though he will do so if there is no other way to encourage them to leave.

If Bertrand is present, Martin will be seen beating the youth and berating him for his lackadaisical devotion to his duties. If the characters do not intervene, Martin will eventually "kill" the groom. He will then shrug, sigh, and look at the characters, saying, "It's hard to find good help these days." Of course, Bertrand will reanimate the next day, like all the household staff who are destroyed. Should the Player Characters intervene, they will find that the servant will not fight on their behalf but will instead attack them. If they do not take sides in the dispute and merely try to discourage the argument, both Martin and Bertrand will put aside their differences and attack.

C6. KENNEL

This small building is the kennel where Lord Joudain kept his five hunting dogs. All of the dogs have since been reanimated through his alchemical experiments with life and death. They are all more or less "alive" now, but looking at them, with their decayed flesh and skeletal features, it is clear that they are not natural in any way. There is a 50% chance that 1d4 of them can be found in the kennel. The remainder of the time the kennel is empty, since the dogs patrol the chateau grounds looking for intruders. The kennel otherwise contains nothing of value.

> **REANIMATED DOGS: Armor 14, 2 Hit Dice, 9hp each, 1 bite for 2d4 damage, Morale 11.** Each successful bite also drains 1 point of Strength; lost Strength points return at a rate of 1 per Turn.

C7. OUTHOUSE

This small wooden structure has a heavy wooden door. Despite that, there is an unpleasant fecal odor emanating from behind it. The smell, while powerful, is not dangerous. Inside the outhouse is a toilet. Should the Random Event roll result in an encounter, the member of the household staff is in fact seated upon the toilet when the characters come upon her.

ground floor

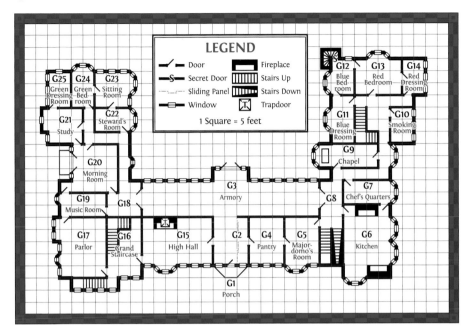

LEGEND

⌐ Door		Fireplace
S Secret Door		Stairs Up
Sliding Panel		Stairs Down
Window		Trapdoor
1 Square = 5 feet		

G25 Green Dressing Room
G24 Green Bedroom
G23 Sitting Room
G22 Steward's Room
G21 Study
G20 Morning Room
G19 Music Room
G18
G17 Parlor
G16 Grand Staircase
G15 High Hall
G2
G4
G5 Pantry
Major-domo's Room
G6 Kitchen
G3 Armory
G8
G7 Chef's Quarters
G9 Chapel
G11 Blue Dressing Room
G10 Smoking Room
G12 Blue Bedroom
G13 Red Bedroom
G14 Red Dressing Room
G1 Porch

G1. PORCH

hen first approached, the metal-reinforced, heavy wooden door leading into Room G2 of this floor is half-open. The door has no lock or bar. However, after all the Player Characters have passed through it, the door will slam shut with a loud bang. The door is now magically locked, though there is a 25% chance that, upon subsequent visits to this room, the effect will have been removed and the door will stand open once again.

G2. SCREENS PASSAGE

Movable wooden screens bisect this wide corridor, blocking the way toward Room G4 of this floor. The screens are finely painted on the side facing Room G15.

The scenes depict skeletons and rotting human remains dancing, cavorting, and engaging in sexual acts with one another. If they could be moved, the screens are worth at least 1,000sp, though finding a suitable buyer might prove difficult given the obscene nature of the artwork.

G3. THE ARMORY

The Armory is a long, covered walkway that connects the two wings of the chateau. There are double doors at each end and another set in the south wall. The north wall houses many windows, some of which are now cracked but none have shattered. The windows provide superb light during the daytime hours, giving the entire area a strangely "warm" quality, unlike much of the rest of the chateau. Black and white checkered tiles of marble cover the floor.

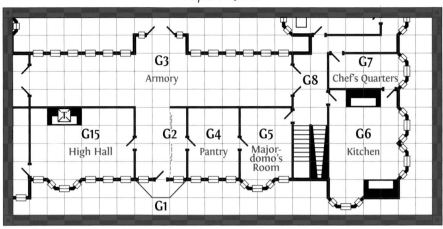

1 square = 5 feet

Despite its name, the Armory contains little in the way of weapons and armor, except for three suits of plate spaced evenly along the north wall between the windows. These suits are completely harmless but are usable and worth 1,500sp each, because of their fine manufacture.

Along the south wall are three richly appointed wooden chairs and two armoires (worth between 500 and 1,000sp each). If anyone enters the Armory unaccompanied by Jaume (see p.19) and/or Miqèl (see p.19), these five pieces of furniture acquire a twisted semblance of life, as well as warped "faces" with which they snarl and growl. The furniture attacks until one of several conditions are met: the Player Characters flee the Armory, the furniture is destroyed in combat, or the furniture fails a Morale Check (in which case it reverts to an inanimate state and will not spring to life again).

> **ANIMATED FURNITURE: Armor 14, Move 30', 3 Hit Dice, 20hp each, 1 grab or bite attack for 1d6 damage, Morale 10.**

G4. PANTRY

Shelves line the walls of this room, which hold sacks and glass jars containing dried and preserved foodstuffs, among other victuals. Now, the sacks and jars are mostly empty. There are, however, a couple of pans, one of which contains bits of tough but still pliable rat meat, which is the primary ingredient Hervisse (see p.19) uses in preparing meals for Bernat (see p.64). The second pan contains fresher—though still tough—meat that is unmistakably that of human beings. This meat was obtained from the corpses of several travelers who had the misfortune to die while in the chateau. Hervisse managed to save some of their flesh from Estève, Laurensa, and Rixenda (see p.18, 21, and 22), who are always on the prowl for sources of fresh meals.

G5. MAJORDOMO'S ROOM

Landri, Joudain's majordomo (see p.20), dwelt here during his life. Even now, there is a 50% chance that he can be found in this chamber, which includes a bed, a writing desk and chair, a chest of drawers, and a small fireplace. The chest of drawers is now largely empty, except for some scraps of rotted cloth.

G6. KITCHEN

The large kitchen contains two food preparation tables, as well as many counter tops, shelves, and cupboards. There is evidence of meals having been prepared in the kitchen recently (wet stains on cutting boards, scraps of meat, etc.). Looking around the kitchen also reveals broken and chipped housewares, some of which rest in a washbasin filled with dirty water. A more careful search reveals a false bottom in the drawer of one of the cupboards containing a treasure map to a cache buried outside the chateau's grounds. The cache consists of a coffer of gems (worth 10,000sp) stolen from Lord Joudain by Hervisse (see p.19) while he was still alive.

The kitchen contains two fireplaces and a fire pit. Only the fire pit is currently lit and above it there is nevertheless a bubbling cauldron. The cauldron gives off a foul odor that is noticeable as soon as anyone enters the room. The contents of the cauldron are hard to discern until a character gets close to it, at which point she will see that it is filled with a clear gelatinous substance. Despite its unpleasant smell, the gelatin (made from the bones and skin of rats and other vermin) is edible and even healthful, healing 1d6+1 points of damage in addition to making the consumer exude the same foul odor as the gelatin itself (-2 reaction from living NPCs). Only *Remove Curse* can undo this effect. There is enough gelatin in the cauldron for ten "meals," but its effects, both good and bad, can be gained only once per consumer.

There is a set of stairs just outside the kitchen that lead to the Wine Cellar (see p.68) and onwards to the Servant's Quarters in the basement (see p.70). The door atop the stairs is locked and the key is in the possession of Landri (see p.20). Lord Joudain's signet ring (found in Room U8 of the upper floor, see p.60) will also open the lock, should the Player Characters possess it. There is a 75% chance that Hervisse is present in this room, hastily preparing a meal or obsessively cleaning. Unless the characters disturb his activities in any way or if they annoy Mondette (see p.22), he will take no notice of them. If the characters find the treasure map mentioned above and present it to him, Hervisse will seize it greedily and immediately turn to dust, as will the treasure map. If this happens, Hervisse is permanently destroyed and cannot be reanimated. Such a turn of events will annoy Joudain greatly, leading to an immediate roll on the Random Event table (see p.8).

Mondette is always present in the kitchen, sitting in a chair along the eastern wall of the room. Between bouts of staring longingly out the window, during which she is insensate to anything else, she berates her husband, telling him to "work faster," "stop wasting time," and similar things. When in this latter state (50% of the time), she will also yell at any characters who enter the kitchen, telling them to "get out" because they are "not supposed to be here." If they do not immediately take heed of her commands, she will order Hervisse (if also present) to deal with them and he will attack. Mondette will not shift from her chair unless she herself is attacked, even if Hervisse is destroyed. If Hervisse is not present, she will still loudly yell and insult the characters, which has a 30% chance of summoning Jaume and Miqèl to the kitchen, who will then attack.

G7. CHEF'S QUARTERS

Hervisse and Mondette lived here in life, but it is now mostly uninhabited. If Hervisse is not present in the kitchen, he will be here, pacing back and forth as he visibly tries to remember something. In this state, he is easily agitated. Should anyone touch him or even talk to him, he will fly into a rage and attack. Other than Hervisse, the room contains only a bed and a chest of drawers.

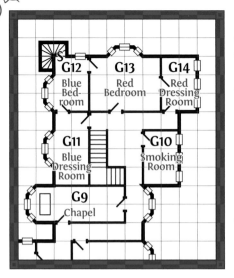

G8. ANTECHAMBER

Once richly furnished and decorated, the finery of this small area has long since moldered away, leaving it bereft of almost anything of real value. Besides shattered plaster and the bones of small animals, the only thing of interest that remains is the Ayarai family crest, which hangs from the east wall. The crest includes the Latin motto Non Omnis Moriar—"I will not wholly die"—which has proven unexpectedly prophetic in the case of Joudain.

G9. CHAPEL OF ST. AZÉDERAC DE XIMES

Originally dedicated to the early 4th-century martyr, Saint Nectarius, Lord Joudain expanded and refurbished the family chapel despite being an unbeliever and a blasphemer. In the process, he had it re-dedicated to a 13th century bishop of Ximes whose canonization was controversial, owing to longstanding (but unsubstantiated) rumors that he was a black magician rather than a pious son of the Church. Through his own research, Joudain became convinced that the rumors of Azéderac's perfidy were true. He sought out relics associated with the bishop (see below) and enshrined them here, occasionally employing some of them in profane rites he performed in the chapel (see p.48) and in his sanctum (see p.60).

The chapel's re-dedication was nominal only; the only Masses celebrated here were black ones. The floor in front of the altar shows signs of a brownish staining, the result of Joudain's having slain Landri (see p.20) here. There are also two reliquaries, one on the north wall and one on the south. Each holds a relic associated with St. Azédarac.

The reliquary on the north wall contains the saint's episcopal miter. Wearing the miter grants a +3 bonus to a Magic-User's Domination roll when casting the 1st-level spell Summon. However, each time the spell is cast, there is a percentage chance equal to the wearer's Charisma score that the next spell cast will act as Summon, regardless of the original spell cast

The reliquary on the south wall contains the skeletal remains of the saint's blessing fingers—his index and middle fingers—which were severed from his hand

by an angry mob who accused Azédarac of being a black magician (which, of course, he was). Possession of the two fingers grants the possessor 1d6+1 points to allocate to any future die rolls (to-hit, saving throws, etc.), except damage rolls. These points are used on a one-for-one basis and can be used either by the possessor of the blessing fingers or by anyone else she designates. This ability can be used once each day. However, each time this ability is used, there is a cumulative 1% chance that the fingers on the caster's right hand will become blackened, shrivel, and fall off.

G10. SMOKING ROOM

The door to this room is locked and trapped. The lock requires Lord Joudain's signet ring, which acts as a key, to open it. The ring can be found on Joudain's body in area U8 (see p.60). The trap is a poisoned needle that injects anyone who attempts to tamper with the lock with a virulent poison. A failed saving throw results in immediate death, while a successful one causes the character to be affected by a powerful hallucinogen for 1d10 Rounds. While under its effects, the character sees her friends as foes and will attack them with the intention of killing them, and without regard for her own safety.

The small chamber beyond is where Lord Joudain entertained his closest friends and associates, debating the meaninglessness of life while imbibing exotic intoxicants of every description. On the walls hang tattered paintings

depicting lurid and degenerate scenes of human misery. If sold to a connoisseur of such depravity, they could fetch as much as 2,000sp, but finding such an individual would no doubt bring with it problems of its own. The room's other furnishings are luxurious, if dusty and worn with age. Transporting them from the chateau would undoubtedly be difficult, but, if a means could be found to do so, they might sell to collectors of antiques for another 3,000sp or more.

Within the smoking room are all manner of liquors and spirits, some from far-off locales and others whose names are unknown to all but the most dedicated aficionados of such beverages. Most remain quite potable—and potent—even after the decades they have rested here. A few have spoiled but none are poisonous or otherwise dangerous. Together, this collection of obscure alcohols might command up to 500sp to those with a taste for such things.

The chamber also contains an ornate humidor (worth approximately 100sp) inside of which still rests a dozen carefully rolled cigars. Strangely, they appear fresh to the touch and smell, despite the many decades since they were likely made. Anyone who chooses to light one and draws its smoke into her mouth must make a successful saving throw against Paralyzation or be turned to stone. Anyone who makes the saving throw feels relaxed and rejuvenated, regaining 1d12 hit points.

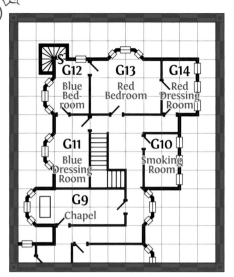

G14. RED DRESSING ROOM

The walls of this room are painted the same shade of red as those of Room G13. The room is otherwise empty, though there is evidence that there were once furnishings here.

G15. HIGH HALL

The high hall contains a wooden table long enough to seat thirty people comfortably. The table is still in the room, as are twenty chairs. The other ten chairs are broken up into fragments and scattered about the room. Chewed bones (mostly from rats) and bits of gristle are piled upon the table, which has dark brown stains in spatters across its length. The room contains a fireplace along the north wall; the remains of a chandelier hang from the high ceiling above. Like the Armory (see p.45), black and white checkered tiles of marble cover the floor. Carved wooden panels cover the walls, depicting flowers and geometric patterns. High up, along the east and west walls, are windows through which those on the upper floor could view the hall below. The western window is much larger, since it is located in an area that Lord Joudain sometimes used as a musicians' gallery, when he wished to entertain his guests in this fashion.

If examined more closely, the characters can see that there appears to be a passageway beneath the grating of the fireplace. Indeed, the grating has hinges, enabling it to be used as a trapdoor. Anyone with a Strength score of 13 or more can easily lift the grating, which leads to a narrow (but nevertheless navigable) passageway that descends 20 feet into the basement (location B4, p.70). There is a 50% chance that the high hall is currently inhabited by three members of the household staff, sitting at the table, eating the meat of rats or (if there have been any

G11. BLUE DRESSING ROOM

The walls of this room are painted blue. There are several wooden armoires here, all of which are largely empty. One armoire contains a silver brooch in the shape of a scarab and crescent moon. The brooch is engraved with an exotic cursive script that looks like Arabic but is in fact completely undecipherable even to *Comprehend Languages*. The brooch is worth 250sp simply on the basis of its materials.

G12. BLUE BEDROOM

The walls of this room are painted the same shade of blue as those of Room G11. The room is well illuminated by a window on the north wall and a large bay window on the west wall. The shattered remains of a wooden bed can be found here. A door in the north wall leads to a staircase to Room U9 on the upper floor (see p.62).

G13. RED BEDROOM

The walls of this room are painted red.
There is a single bay window on the north wall and a bare bed against the west wall.

unfortunate travelers in the area recently) human beings. These three members are Estève, Laurensa, and Rixenda (see p. 18, 21, and 22). If they are not here, they are in the basement and will react to the sounds of anyone moving the grating in the fireplace by ascending the passageway to investigate. They move silently while doing so, which increases their chance of surprise to a roll of 1–3 on 1d6.

G16. GRAND STAIRCASE

The staircase is carved entirely of wood. Its posts are surmounted by tarasques (lion-headed dragons with six legs, turtle shells, and barbed tails) holding shields bearing the Ayarai coat of arms. The bottom of the stairs is barred by a short wooden gate intended to prevent Lord Joudain's dogs (see p.53) from ascending the stairs to reach the bedrooms. Each time the characters pass through this area, there is a 25% that one of the dogs will be here,

resting (unless all the dogs have been destroyed beforehand). The dog will attack anyone approaching it, but, if the gate is opened, it will desist and immediately run up the stairs with obvious glee across its decaying face.

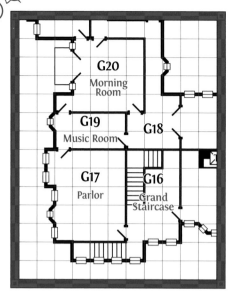

G20
Morning
Room

G19
Music Room

G18

G17
Parlor

G16
Grand
Staircase

G17. PARLOR

The parlor is where Lord Joudain greeted guests and conversed with them while they waited for dinner to be served in the nearby high hall. The room contains the remnants of many luxurious chairs and sofas. The curtains and other decorations are similarly damaged and decaying. The only items in the room immune to the passage of time are three different portraits of Lord Joudain, each one depicting him at different ages—as a child, as a youth, and as he was at the time shortly before his suicide. These portraits hang on the north, west, and south walls and show no signs either of damage or age. They are firmly ensconced on the walls and cannot be easily removed by any normal means without also damaging the walls on which they hang. Removal of a portrait destroys any magical qualities it possesses (see below) and angers Lord Joudain, resulting in an immediate roll on the Joudain's Fun table.

If any character stares intently at one or more of the portraits for longer than a minute, there is a possibility she may gain a bonus or suffer a penalty. The characteristics of each portrait are as follows:

CHILDHOOD PORTRAIT (North Wall):
This portrait shows a young boy with long, curly, blond hair dressed in blue velvet clothing. He is seated in a large, cushioned chair and has several dogs arrayed at his feet. One small dog rests on the boy's lap. If the youngest character in the party stares at the portrait, she must make a saving throw versus Magic. If successful, nothing happens, but if the saving throw is failed, the character's hair turns blond (if it was not already) and she gains the ability to comprehend and communicate with ordinary animals once per day. Characters other than the youngest who stare at the portrait gain no bonuses or penalties from doing so.

YOUTHFUL PORTRAIT (West Wall):
This portrait shows a somewhat effeminate looking adolescent male with long, curly hair of a slightly darker shade than that of the child in the previous portrait. The youth is dressed in black silken clothes and wears a rapier at his belt. He has a strange smirk on his face and his eyes seem to stare directly at the viewer. The first male character to stare at the portrait permanently gains 1 point to his Charisma score but loses 1 from his Wisdom score. No ability may be raised above 18 or below 3 in this manner. Subsequent male characters or any female characters who stare at the portrait gain neither bonuses nor penalties from doing so.

ADULT PORTRAIT (South Wall): This portrait shows a middle-aged man with shorter, wavy brown-but-graying hair. He is dressed in green and brown garments and carries a rod in his hand. The rod is topped with a horned, demonic face. The man looks thin, slightly ill, and wears a bored expression on his face. If the oldest character in the party stares at the portrait, she must make a saving throw versus Magic. If successful nothing happens, but if the saving throw is failed, the character's hair turns white (if it was not already) and she is cursed with the desire to end her life. Until *Remove Curse* is cast on the character, she will show no concern for her well-being, even in dangerous situations. She will rush headlong into mêlée, enter rooms without first checking for traps, etc.

G18. ANTECHAMBER

Once richly furnished and decorated, the finery of this small area has long since moldered away, leaving it bereft of almost anything of real value. Besides shattered plaster and the bones of small animals, the only thing of interest that remains is the Ayarai family crest, which hangs from the west wall. The crest includes the Latin motto Non Omnis Moriar—"I will not wholly die"—which has proven unexpectedly prophetic in the case of Joudain.

G19. MUSIC ROOM

Six fine but rotting chairs can be found here, in addition to a harpsichord and its bench. The harpsichord, though in ill repair due to decades of neglect, still works. Playing the harpsichord draws the attention of Landri (see p.20), who comes to the room 1d6 Rounds later. If his reaction is Talkative or Helpful, he will compliment the player of the harpsichord and inquire as to whether she requires anything of him. He will acquiesce to one request to the best of his ability, though his knowledge is limited. If asked, for example, how to escape from the chateau, Landri will reply, "Entertain my lord" or something to that effect, but he will provide no more specifics. If his reaction is Unfriendly or Hostile, he will summon Jaume and Miqèl (see p.19), assuming they have not been destroyed, to "toss these ruffians out." An indifferent reaction results in his simply poking his head into the room briefly, frowning disapprovingly, and returning to his own room.

G20. MORNING ROOM

A large couch, four chairs, and a small table are present in this room, which also contains a beautiful tapestry depicting mythological and legendary creatures, albeit ones of decidedly sinister cast (anthropophagic ogres and giants, dragons, demons, etc.). The room also contains more than two dozen portraits of young women on its walls, all of which have been defaced in some way (the canvas cut with a knife, the paint smeared with dark stains, etc.). There is a set of heavy wooden double doors on the western wall that lead outside the chateau. When the room is first entered these doors are magically locked, but there is a 50% chance that the next time the room is entered the effect is no longer active.

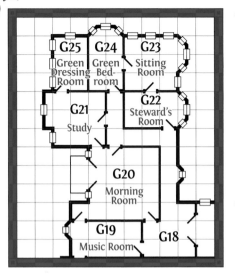

- *De Occulta Philosophia libri III:* This Latin text is less than a century old and was written by the German magician Heinrich Cornelius Agrippa. The work's three books deal with elemental, celestial, and intellectual magic. The copy in the study contains Joudain's marginal notes (in Latin and Occitan), which suggest that he did not think much of Agrippa's erudition. The book is worth 75sp to collectors and the curious, and twice that to Magic-Users.

- *Picatrix:* This book is written in Latin, but is partially a translation of an earlier Arabic work. Its primary subject matter is astrology, though there are sections devoted to many other occult topics. The book is worth 150sp to collectors and the curious, and twice that to Magic-Users.

G21. STUDY

The doors to the study are locked and can be opened by Joudain's signet ring, just like the Smoking Room (see p.49). The study contains an oaken table, a chair, a writing desk with its own chair, and many shelves on which can be found dusty or moldering books and paper. Most of the books have had their pages torn out, which lie scattered about the room haphazardly. The books and papers are mostly unremarkable, with a couple of exceptions (see below). Most are historical and religious texts of a mundane sort. If the characters take the time to sort through the mess of pages (and if the Referee so decides), one or more of them might hold some scrap of information about either Lord Joudain's personal history or some other topic of interest to the Player Characters. Lord Joudain was truly catholic in his interests, so it is not inconceivable that the study might contain a useful (but non-magical) book or scroll. Joudain's mundane books are worth 600sp in total, if taken and sold to interested parties. The two noteworthy books in the study, both of which are still in good condition, are:

Beside the writing desk is a waste paper basket, inside of which is seethes a grayish-white mass of what appears to be crumpled and torn handwritten pages. The ink on the pages is smeared and mostly illegible. Should anyone approach the basket closely or touch it (even at a distance), the mass pours out with the sound of crinkling paper and attacks. The mass exists only partially in this reality, so sections of it fade in and out of view along the creases made in the individual papers.

The mass is the physical manifestation of Lord Joudain's anger and frustration at finding nothing within the books in this room to alleviate his boredom. Initially, the mass attacks the character who disturbed it, but after the first Round of combat it focuses its attention on the closest spell casting character. It will continue to attack that character above all others until destroyed, unless another spellcaster comes closer. The mass will leave the study to pursue characters who flee.

MASS OF PAPERS: Armor 12, Move 30', 5 Hit Dice, 32hp, one slam doing 1d6 damage, Morale 12. Any spellcaster struck by the mass must make a saving throw versus Magic or have a single spell of the lowest level she can cast stripped from her mind. This heals the mass by 1d6 per level of the spell. Spells cast at the mass have no effect (except those that produce or mimic fire effects) and increase its hit dice (and hit points) by 1 per spell level. The mass takes double damage from non-magical fire.

G22. STEWARD'S ROOM

Elias (see p.17) dwelled here in life. There is a 75% chance that he will be here should the characters enter it, unless he has been previously destroyed. If so, he will be found sitting at his small desk, hunched over a ledger book filled with figures. Unless disturbed, he will not take notice of the characters. If disturbed, roll on the reaction table. If Indifferent, he simply ignores the characters. If Unfriendly or Hostile, he attacks them, all the while screaming for Jaume and Miqèl (see p.19) to come to his aid (30% chance). If Talkative or Helpful, he begins an interview with the characters, asking them about their qualifications for employment at the chateau, the sort of salary they expect, and how much they know about Lord Joudain and his activities. Like all the inhabitants of the chateau, Elias's information is both limited and out of date, but he will nevertheless correct any misapprehensions the characters might possess about Joudain, the chateau, etc. Once he has finished his interview, he will state that "someone will inform you of the Master's decision at a later date" and will return to his work.

G23. SITTING ROOM

Shattered chairs and a table can be found here.

G24. GREEN BEDROOM

The walls of this room are painted green. The remains of a bed can be found here, as well as a large bay window on the north wall. The ceiling has numerous water stains on it, as well as evidence that portions may be rotten.

G25. GREEN DRESSING ROOM

The walls of this room are painted the same shade of green as those of Room 24. There are two chests of drawers here, in addition to a large free-standing closet. There is nothing of value in any of them. The ceiling shows patches of water staining.

upper floor

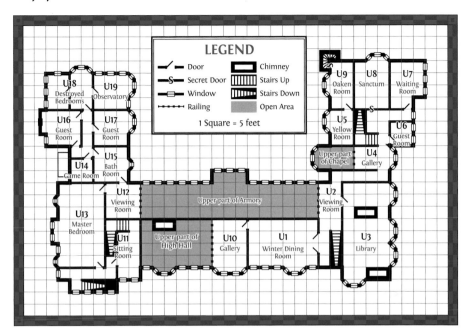

LEGEND

Door	Chimney
Secret Door	Stairs Up
Window	Stairs Down
Railing	Open Area

1 Square = 5 feet

U18 Destroyed Bedrooms
U19 Observatory
U16 Guest Room
U17 Guest Room
U15 Bath Room
U14 Game Room
U12 Viewing Room
U13 Master Bedroom
U11 Sitting Room
Upper part of High Hall
U10 Gallery
U1 Winter Dining Room
Upper part of Armory
U2 Viewing Room
U3 Library
U9 Oaken Room
U8 Sanctum
U7 Waiting Room
U5 Yellow Room
U6 Guest Room
Upper part of Chapel
U4 Gallery

U1. WINTER DINING ROOM

HE DOORS TO THE WINTER dining room are both locked. The room beyond contains a large wooden table and seating for ten. Both the table and the chairs are well preserved, though covered with dust. The room is not otherwise noteworthy.

U2. VIEWING ROOM

The western wall of this room possesses three wooden, sliding windows through which an observer can look down on the Armory (see p.45) below.

U3. LIBRARY

The door to this room has been flung open, revealing that it has seemingly been ransacked. Books and papers lie scattered about the room and several bookcases have been knocked over, creating a scene of chaos. This is Lord Joudain's "public" library, which is to say, the library he allowed strangers and guests to see. As such, like his study on the ground floor (see p.54), it is largely filled only with fairly ordinary tomes, though there are many more of them here—literally hundreds. Though probably of little immediate interest to the characters, many might be valuable to collectors and antiquarians, if they could be transported.

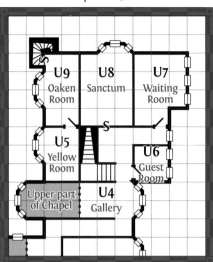

1 square = 5 feet

Spending at least two Turns examining the room reveals that the library contains books on almost any non-arcane subject. Many of the books have suffered age damage, are worm-eaten, or having missing pages; but, as noted above, there are hundreds of volumes here and the well-maintained ones outnumber the dilapidated.

U4. GALLERY

This room looks down on the chapel (see p.48), providing additional seating for worshipers who could not be accommodated below. It also provides a better view of the intricate artwork of the chapel's coffer ceiling and stained glass windows. From this height, smaller details, such as depictions of demons, are visible that cannot be easily seen from the ground floor. Indeed, a careful examination from this height reveals many other trompe-l'œil features, which gives the chapel an entirely new cast There is a 25% chance that Landri may be found here, seemingly praying on his knees. He will immediately take note of the characters' presence and will ask them to join him in prayer. If they agree, he will offer a short prayer in Latin to St. Nectarius, the original patron of the chapel, asking him for his blessing and intercession. He then gets up and leaves, returning to his room. If the characters do not agree, he sneers and rebukes them, which causes the character with the highest Wisdom in the party to suffer a -1 penalty to all saving throws until *Remove Curse* is cast or the character seeks out Landri and apologizes to him for her "impiety."

If she has not been encountered elsewhere or destroyed, Clareta (see p.17) can be found here, attempting in vain to clean up the mess. Being wholly insubstantial, she cannot touch the books, no matter how hard she tries. When the characters enter, she looks up at them with an exasperated expression and asks, "Can you help me? The Master will be here soon and he hates it when his books aren't put away." Her spectral form visibly shudders and fades briefly out of existence as she says the second sentence. If the characters then attempt to assist her by putting books and/or bookcases back into their "proper" places—Clareta no longer remembers where they truly belong; all that is important is that they not be on the floor—she will smile and then disappear. For as long as they are in the chateau, so long as they do not make a mess or otherwise disturb the contents of a room, she will not attack them. However, if the characters ignore her pleas or outright refuse to assist her, she will fly into a rage and attack.

U5. YELLOW ROOM

The walls of this room are painted a particularly vibrant shade of yellow. The walls have been vandalized, however. Someone has crudely drawn a variety of geometric shapes on them through the use of a black pigment of some sort. There is no furniture in the room.

U6. GUEST BEDROOM

Lord Joudain used this bedroom to house guests who stayed at the chateau. On one occasion, he entertained a rival in the black arts, whom he whimsically slew by means of a poison that both prevented the rival's body from decay and allowed it to retain the outward appearance of life, although it does not breathe nor does it have a heartbeat or pulse. The Magic-User had summoned an aerial entity which was bound to protect him from harm while he slept.

Because of the poison's peculiar effect, the entity still believes its master to be alive but asleep and will attack anyone who enters the room and looks as if she might harm him. Approaching the preserved body alone is not sufficient provocation, but attempting to loot his jewelry or other possessions is. The black magician wears a ring worth 700sp solely on the basis of its materials. If worn, the ring reflects any spell or spell-like effect targeted on the wearer back at its original caster, but only once, after which the ring is simply a normal (if valuable) piece of jewelry. He also has a purse in which he has three gems, each one worth 250sp. The entity will fight until either it is destroyed or the "attacks" against its master cease. Anyone taking an item from the body will be attacked until dead or the stolen item is returned to the body.

AERIAL ENTITY: Armor (see below), Move 240', 5 Hit Dice, 29hp, 2 immaterial tentacles for 1d6 damage each, Morale 12. Immune to normal attacks, first attack against creature always misses, vulnerable to silver (takes +1 damage per die).

On a table near the bed is the rival's last meal: a plate with some chicken bones and a glass, inside of which rests a liquid looking very much like wine. The liquid is in fact the potion Joudain gave to his guest. Because of its magical nature, it has retained both its liquid state and its potency, despite being left to the elements for so long. If anyone drinks the potion, she must make a saving throw versus Poison. Failure results in death—though, like the rival, the imbiber's body does not decay and is in fact perfectly preserved, even years after her demise.

U7. WAITING ROOM

A half-dozen chairs are found in this wood-paneled room, in addition to two small tables. The room is otherwise unremarkable.

U8. SANCTUM

The door to this room is not only hidden but also locked and trapped. The lock can be opened by Joudain's signet ring—which, unfortunately for the characters, can be found inside the secret room itself. The trap is magical in nature and, if set off, creates a blast of energy that inflicts 5d6 points of damage to all creatures within a 10-foot radius. Lawful characters get no saving throw to avoid the damage, whereas Neutral characters may save versus Magic to take half damage. Chaotic characters may make a save to avoid all damage entirely.

Within this hidden room, Lord Joudain practiced the dark rites he hoped might give him insight into the true nature of the universe, or at least alleviate his boredom. The room is decorated with images of leering demons and other blasphemous beings. There are likewise many implements used in conjuration, summoning, and necromancy. Taken from this room, these implements might command as much as 1,000sp from Magic-Users or those interested in demon worship. One of these implements is an ornate iron dagger that, if it successfully strikes a demon, banishes it to the Beyond immediately. The dagger is destroyed in the process of so striking a demon, however. Unsurprisingly, Lawful characters feel extremely uneasy in this room, suffering a -1 penalty to all attack and saving throw rolls while they remain here.

In addition to the aforementioned implements, the sanctum contains Joudain's collection of magical texts. Two books in that collection are noteworthy:

- *Liber Juratus Honorii:* The book is written in Latin by a magician using the name Honorius of Thebes. The book consists of 93 different chapters in which it teaches a variety of charms, spells, and conjurations, including how to summon and bind demons. Reading the book grants any Magic-User a +1 bonus to her saving throw versus Magic when casting the spell *Summon*. The book is worth 200sp to collectors and the curious, and twice that to Magic-Users.

- *Livre des Esperitz:* The book is written in French and purports to be a translation from an earlier Hebrew work composed by King Solomon. Strictly speaking, the book is not a grimoire, as it does not include any spells whatsoever. Instead, it is an extensive catalog of the demonic beings, including many great princes of Hell. Bayemon (see below) is not listed amongst these beings. The book is worth 100sp to collectors and the curious, and twice that to Magic-Users.

The collection also includes Lord Joudain's spellbook. In life, Joudain was an 11th-level Magic-User. His spellbook thus contains spells up to the 6th level. The Referee should choose which spells to include in the spellbook, based on what he wishes to include in his own campaign.

This secret room is also where Lord Joudain committed suicide, spilling his blood into a large basin that contained numerous magical herbs and chemicals. He hoped that this ritual would not only end his life but allow his consciousness to roam freely through the cosmos. Unfortunately, he misunderstood the nature of the ritual he was attempting and so bound himself to the grounds of his chateau. Lord Joudain's now-mummified corpse lies on the ground beside the basin, dressed in a silk robe covered with occult symbols. He has nothing of value on his person except a gold amulet worth 1,500sp and a signet ring that, in addition to opening various locked rooms in the chateau, is worth 1,000sp in its own right.

In the center of the room is an unbroken summoning circle in which can be found a demon named Bayemon. Lord Joudain summoned the demon shortly before he lost interest in mortal existence and committed suicide, binding Bayemon here for the last few decades with no means of escape. The demon will attempt to trick the characters into freeing it by breaking the summoning circle (by erasing one of its chalk outlines, etc.), offering them anything they wish in return for this service. Bayemon explains (truthfully, as it turns out) that it is utterly powerless until the circle is broken and thus cannot grant the characters their reward until it is freed. Once freed, the demon attacks the characters, hoping to destroy them utterly in recompense for so many years of entrapment. While within the circle, Bayemon is immune to both physical and magical attacks; it can only be harmed if the circle is broken.

BAYEMON: Armor 16, Move 90', 7 Hit Dice, 32hp, 2 claw attacks for 1d6 damage each, 1 bite attack for 1d8 damage plus poison (save or die), Morale 12. Can cast *Darkness* at will. Any creature slain by the demon cannot be restored to life by any means.

1 square = 5 feet

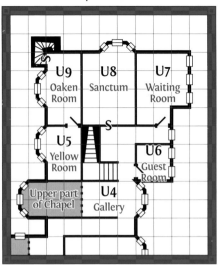

U9. OAKEN ROOM

So called because its floors and wood-paneled walls are made from oak, this room is also a favorite haunt of Guilhèm the page (see p.18). There is a 75% chance that he will be found in this room, if he has not yet been encountered elsewhere or destroyed. Guilhèm spends his time here staring out the large window on the western wall, looking at the site of the former gardens.

When the characters enter this room, he immediately turns to greet them, asking them to join him in admiring "the beauty of the garden." If the characters do this, he will ask them what they think of the (non-existent) flowers and shrubs. Should they lie by claiming to see them or otherwise give an indication that they are simply playing along with the undead boy, he will chide them, saying, "I know they're gone, you know; there's no need to patronize me." If the characters point out that the flowers are gone or that they cannot see them, Guilhèm will smile and sigh happily, "Finally, someone who sees things as they truly are." This act grants the Player Characters the benefits of *Protection from Evil, 10' Radius* for the next Turn.

Attacking Guilhèm results in a roll on the Random Event table (see p.8). Guilhèm will attempt to flee from the room and seek out Jaume and Miqèl (see p.19) for protection. Should anyone destroy Guilhèm, in addition to the penalties to Joudain's Fun noted on p.27, she merits Joudain's special ire. All subsequent negative results from the Random Event table target that character first and foremost for the rest of the time she is in the chateau.

U10. GALLERY

This chamber contains a collection of three paintings, a large stained glass window, and a screen that enables occupants to look down onto the Great Hall below (see p.50). The paintings all depict bucolic scenes but are otherwise not noteworthy. There is also a desiccated corpse standing in front of the stained glass window, its clothing almost rotted away. The corpse carries a sword, a silver dagger, and a backpack devoid of any contents.

The stained glass window depicts an intricately arranged garden, full of vibrant flowers, bushes, and trees. Looking carefully at it also reveals tiny moving figures that occasionally appear from among the foliage. The figures face the viewer and appear to be saying something but no sound emanates from their mouths. Some of them also make motions or gestures that suggest they are encouraging the viewer to flee. At that point, the Referee should call for a saving throw versus Magic by anyone looking at the window. Those who save successfully are unaffected. Those who fail swap their bodies with one of the other viewers who also failed. This effect can be dispelled as usual.

If only one character fails her saving throw or if there are an uneven number of characters who failed, any "left over" characters find their life forces trapped within the window and their original bodies slain. This effect can be dispelled by magical means, but, without a new body for each trapped life force to inhabit, it will simply dissipate and the character is truly lost forever. Removing or damaging the window immediately releases all the life forces held within it.

U11. SITTING ROOM

This area at the top of the stairs contains three chairs whose cushions have long since rotted away.

U12. VIEWING ROOM

The eastern wall of this room possesses three wooden, sliding windows through which an observer can look down on the Armory (see p.45) below.

(Map labels: 14 Room, Bath Room, U12 Viewing Room, 13 ster oom, Upper part of Armory, U11 Sitting Room, Upper part of High Hall, U10 Gallery)

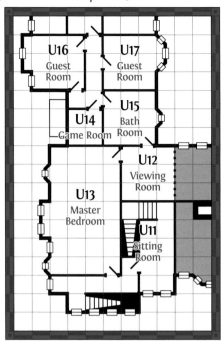

1 square = 5 feet

U16 — Guest Room
U17 — Guest Room
U15 — Bath Room
U14 — Game Room
U12 — Viewing Room
U13 — Master Bedroom
U11 — Sitting Room

U13. MASTER BEDROOM

Even in its somewhat dilapidated state, the master bedroom is beautiful. There are two large windows on the western wall, as well as a balcony (which opens freely, even when other doors in the chateau are under the effects of *Wizard Lock*). There is also a large fireplace set into the eastern wall. The walls themselves are decorated with wood carvings, bas-reliefs, and tapestries, most of which are strangely well-maintained. Unlike most of the other rooms in the chateau, the master bedroom is free of dust or cobwebs. If it is winter or simply cold, there is also a fire in the fireplace.

The reason for this is that it is currently occupied by a middle-aged man who looks somewhat like the man in the adult portrait hanging on the wall of Room G17 of the lower level (see p.52). Despite appearances, this is not in fact Lord Joudain returned from the dead. Rather, it is Bernat, the sole survivor of a previous expedition into the chateau. Joudain's consciousness found the man's broad resemblance to his mortal form amusing and so instructed his undead servants to treat Bernat as if he were in fact the chateau's master.

> **BERNAT:** Armor 12, Move 120',
> 1st Level Fighter, 9hp, 1 fist attack
> for 1d4 damage, Morale 10.

Bernat now spends most of his time in this bedroom, waited on hand and foot by Landri and the other household servants, who provide him with a regular supply of the finest meats from rats and other small creatures as they can find, occasionally supplemented with the flesh of travelers who die on the grounds and whose corpses are not stolen away by the other servants in the basement beneath the chateau. Because of his diet of human flesh, Bernat is slowly becoming less than human in appearance, as the years crawl on, but he has also gained functional immortality—a process that has claimed his sanity as well.

Bernat does his best to play the part of Lord Joudain but even a few moments of conversation with him reveals how utterly mad he is. Provided the characters play along, Bernat is quite content to entertain them with stories of his imagined life as lord of the chateau. He will even go so far as to offer them a tour of the place, summoning Jaume and Miqèl (see p.19), if they have not yet been destroyed, to accompany them for as long as they require. Bernat will never leave the master bedroom himself, claiming that he is "simply too busy with his correspondence" to be able to do so. He will then point to his writing desk, which is piled with papers, ink pots, envelopes, and the like.

The moment any character draws attention to anything that suggests Bernat is not in fact Joudain, he grows angry and attacks the characters, calling on "his" servants to aid him. Provided they have not already been destroyed, Landri, Elias, Jaume, and Miqèl arrive in 1d4 Rounds to defend Bernat. Aside from the opulent furnishings of the room (which could easily fetch 20,000sp or more, if they could be transported from the chateau) Bernat possesses a large sack containing 3,000sp and an enchanted sword that he uses in combat. The sword once belonged to Lord Joudain himself and only demonstrates its enchantment after it has been used to slay someone living. Once so activated, one point of damage of every strike landed on a target can only be healed by magical means, unless *Remove Curse* is cast on the target.

U14. GAME ROOM

A large wooden table and several chairs can be found here. During Joudain's life, this is where he and his guests might play cards and games of chance.

U15. BATHROOM

This room was used for bathing and contains a large metal tub and a wash-basin. There is also a mirror on the western wall. The mirror is encircled in copper knotwork, which reflects red in any torch or lantern light. It stands about six feet tall, stretching from slightly above the floor to slightly below the ceiling. It is in fact a magical mirror. Anyone who looks into it sees a vision of themselves at the time of their death. Like all such magical devices, the Referee needs to be clever in presenting it, simultaneously implying that what it shows is an infallible vision of the future (assuming the Player Characters can figure out what it does) and being vague/flexible enough that that infallibility survives contact with the randomness of dice and player action. Alternately, the Referee might instead decide that the mirror can be passed through, leading to Voivodja, the setting of *A Red & Pleasant Land*, but doing so would certainly change the complexion of this adventure and may not be to everyone's taste.

U16. GUESTROOM

This locked bedroom is now the haunt of Dame Helissente, a mistress of Lord Joudain, who locked herself in this bedroom without either food or water in order to "punish" him for his having taken another lover. Helissente had hoped that Joudain would express his love for her by saving her from wasting away, but, to her surprise and dismay, he found her actions diverting for a time and ordered the room (included its windows) bolted from the outside as well. He took pleasure in listening to Helissente's begging for him to release her from the room, as well as her claims to have forgiven him for his "indiscretion." The jilted mistress eventually died in the bedroom and her vengeful consciousness remains here, mad with grief and rage. She will attack any who enter the room until either she or they are destroyed. Dame Helissente's mortal remains can be found atop the rotting bed. There are two rings on the corpse's fingers, one of which is worth 250sp and other, set with an emerald, is worth 1,000sp.

> **DAME HELISSENTE:** Armor 18, Move 150', 6 Hit Dice, 40hp, one ghostly touch attack doing 1d8 damage plus energy drain (see p.25), Morale 12. Usual undead immunities, unaffected by non-magical or non-silver weapons.

1 square = 5 feet

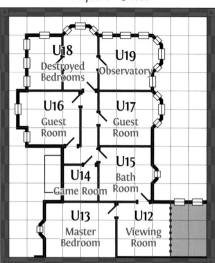

U17. GUESTROOM

This is another guestroom. Its original contents consisted of a bed, a chair, and an armoire. All of these furnishings have since been smashed to pieces, the debris scattered about the room in several piles.

U18. DESTROYED BEDROOMS

The ceilings of these two bedrooms have collapsed, as has part of the outside wall, which has allowed rain and other adverse weather conditions to damage their furnishings. The floors have also been damaged, making them somewhat unsafe to cross. There is a 1 in 6 chance per 10 feet crossed that the floor will collapse, dropping the character into either Room G24 (see p.55) or Room G25 (see p.55) on the lower level. Specialists may substitute their Stealth skill chance if it is greater.

U19. OBSERVATORY

This room served as an observatory during Lord Joudain's life. He had set up a telescope here, along with star charts and other related paraphernalia, all of which are still here. There is also a small library of books on astronomy and astrology, about half of which are damaged due to age, worms, water, etc.

Guilhèm (see p.18) is here, assuming he has not been encountered elsewhere or destroyed previously. He will be using the telescope and will beckon anyone who enters to take his place, saying, "The Master said he sometimes asks questions of the stars—and they answered him! You can ask them, too, if you dare." Any character who looks through the telescope has the option of using it to ask a number of questions of a star. The number is up to the character. All questions are answered with a one-word reply and there is only a 50% chance the answer will be truthful. In addition, there is a 5% chance per question (non-cumulative) that the questioner will become possessed by an astral beast for a number of weeks equal to the number of questions asked.

Attacking Guilhèm results in an immediate roll on the Random Event table (see p.8). Guilhèm will attempt to flee from the room and seek out Jaume and Miqèl for protection. Should anyone destroy Guilhèm, in addition to the penalties to Joudain's Fun noted on p.27, she merits Joudain's special ire. All subsequent negative results from the Random Event table target that character first and foremost for the rest of the time she is in the chateau.

basement

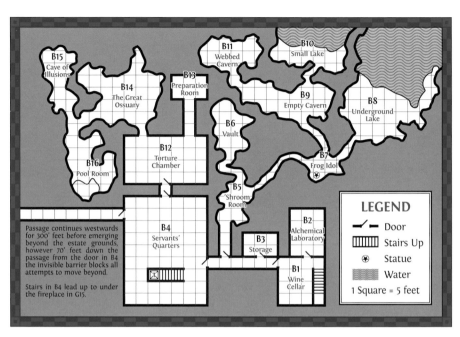

LEGEND

◢ ▬	Door
▥▥▥	Stairs Up
✴	Statue
〜〜	Water
1 Square = 5 feet	

B15 — Cave of Illusions
B14 — The Great Ossuary
B16 — Pool Room
B13 — Preparation Room
B12 — Torture Chamber
B11 — Webbed Cavern
B10 — Small Lake
B9 — Empty Cavern
B8 — Underground Lake
B7 — Frog Idol
B6 — Vault
B5 — 'Shroom Room
B4 — Servants' Quarters
B3 — Storage
B2 — Alchemical Laboratory
B1 — Wine Cellar

Passage continues westwards for 300' feet before emerging beyond the estate grounds, however 70' feet down the passage from the door in B4 the invisible barrier blocks all attempts to move beyond.

Stairs in B4 lead up to under the fireplace in G15.

HE BASEMENT LEVEL OF the chateau consists of both the chambers worked from the stone beneath it, as well as a series of natural caverns that connect to those chambers.

B1. WINE CELLAR

This chamber is not naked rock but is instead carved into a regular shape. When the chateau was inhabited by the living, it served as a wine cellar, as evidenced by the large number of shelves containing bottles of various sorts found herein. Most of these shelves and bottles have since been smashed or otherwise damaged, but a small number have not. There are 18 intact bottles in the cellar, each of which could fetch 10-20sp if sold to a connoisseur in a major urban center.

The room is otherwise empty. The northern and western doors out of this chamber are locked and require the use of either the key possessed by Landri (see p.68) or Lord Joudain's signet ring to open.

B2. ALCHEMICAL LABORATORY

Lord Joudain used this large room to practice alchemy, engaging in research he hoped would alleviate his world-weariness. He spent large sums of money to acquire an impressive collection of chemicals and equipment, but he soon discovered that he lacked the dedication to take up alchemy seriously. Thus, he abandoned the laboratory, allowing it to molder and collect dust behind its locked doors. The lock is not trapped and can be picked. Otherwise, only Lord Joudain's signet ring will open it.

The walls of the laboratory are covered with many shelves, cabinets, hooks, and other storage devices. Inside of them are innumerable vials, bottles, and beakers, each of them filled with liquids and powders, along with many strange tools of use to alchemists. Taken together, the materials here are worth in excess of 2,000sp to those knowledgeable in this field, but transporting it all would prove difficult, at least until the curse on the chateau is lifted.

If anyone chooses to imbibe or consume the contents of any of the vials in the room, roll 1d10 to determine its effects from the adjacent table. Except for the poisonous ones, the following effects are not cumulative. If a character already under an effect drinks another bottle with the same effect, nothing occurs.

B3. STORAGE ROOM

This room contains numerous barrels and crates, which once contained dried foods, fresh water, and other provisions for use in emergencies. All of them are now either smashed or empty. There is nothing of value in the room.

d10	DRINKING FROM THE VIALS
1-2	Poison. Save or die.
3-4	Poison. Save or die at -2.
5	The imbiber turns a bright shade of green but is otherwise unharmed. The color is permanent but can be removed by magic.
6	The imbiber becomes semi-transparent, which grants them a +1 bonus to surprise rolls and decreases the likelihood of their being seen by 25%. As with 5 above, the change is permanent unless removed through magic.
7	The imbiber uncontrollably hiccups for 1d4 Rounds, during which time she cannot attack or defend herself.
8	The imbiber shrinks to 10% her normal height for 1d6 Turns.
9	The imbiber is healed for 1d6+10 points of damage. If the imbiber is not damaged at the time, she instead gains a point of Constitution permanently.
10	Dream Drug. Save versus Poison or fall into a deep slumber for 1d6 Turns, during which time the character's mind leaves her body and enters a nightmarish realm. This realm is inhabited by strange, ethereal beings who seek to wreak havoc in the waking world by possessing the bodies of sleepers. Characters who consume this dream drug must make a saving throw, with a -1 penalty for every Turn the character is asleep. If the character possesses Wisdom and/or Charisma above 13, she gains a +1 bonus to the saving throw (maximum +2 bonus). Failure indicates the character has been possessed and will henceforth attempt to do damage, betray, and otherwise harm her companions for a number of hours equal to the character's level. At the Referee's discretion, certain spells might end the possession sooner.

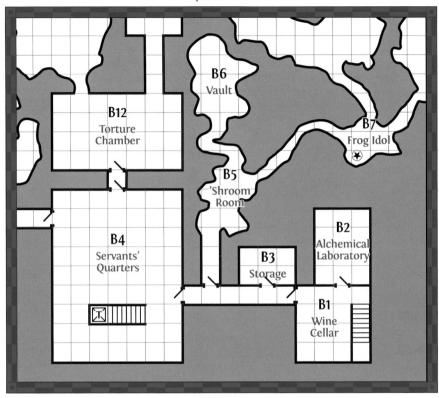

1 square = 5 feet

B4. SERVANTS' QUARTERS

This large room served as the servants' quarters during the lifetime of Lord Joudain. Originally, the servants lived off the grounds of the chateau itself, in a separate wooden building that has long since been destroyed. As his ennui increased, Lord Joudain wanted his servants to live within the walls of the chateau so that they might be readily available should he ever need them for any purpose. These quarters were constructed to house them. The quarters also served as a dining room, where they ate their meals.

The quarters are currently inhabited by those servants that retain a corporeal existence in death. There is a 50% chance that Estève, Laurensa, and Rixenda (see p.18, 21, and 22) are here, if they have not already been encountered elsewhere or destroyed. These servants are extremely territorial and resent the intrusion of anyone into their quarters, attacking them immediately and fighting until either they or their opponents are dead or they break morale—in which case they flee up the passageway that leads to the fireplace in Room G15 (see p.50).

There is some furniture in the room— a large table, several rough chairs, and a couple of folding screens intended to provide some measure of privacy. Behind one of the screens is a tub filled with stagnant water, in which some of the servants continue to "wash," despite their undead state.

Consequently, the water is infected with a disease. Anyone who places their hands within it has a 10% chance of contracting it (and a 20% chance of spreading it to others by physical contact). Any who contract the disease have a 25% chance of lapsing into a coma 1d4 weeks later, half of whom will never awaken, sickening and dying some time later.

In addition to the passageway leading to the high hall, there are three exits from this room. The door to the north is locked and can be opened only by Landri's key or Lord Joudain's signet ring. The door to the west is not locked and leads up to the surface, some 100 yards away from the grounds of the chateau. Unfortunately, it is affected by the curse and anyone who walks more than 40 feet down its length will find themselves blocked by a magical barrier like that which bars most other egress from the chateau's grounds. The third exit leads to the wine cellar and up to the kitchen.

B5. 'SHROOM ROOM

This cavern is damp and musty, giving off an unpleasant odor from some distance away. Its interior is covered in patches of purplish-black mushrooms about 4 to 6 inches in height. These mushrooms sense vibrations and burst forth a cloud of noxious and choking dust when a living—not undead—creature comes within 10 feet. All those in the area must make a saving throw versus Poison or lose 1d6 hit points permanently. Even if the saving throw is successful, an affected creature is stunned for 2d4 rounds from fits of choking and coughing. Cold instantly kills these mushrooms.

There are three patches of mushrooms, one near each of the cave's entrances.

B6. THE VAULT

This chamber appears to be empty, but its contents are hidden by an illusion of a rock wall that can be overcome by anyone who makes a successful saving throw versus Magic. Those who save will see two chests and three coffers in the southeast corner of the room. The two chests are locked, while the coffers are not. None of them are trapped.

- Chest #1 contains 3,000sp.
- Chest #2 contains 1,000sp, 3 gems (each worth 200sp), and a necklace (worth 250sp).
- Coffer #1 contains a cursed brooch that afflicts the wearer with a wasting disease that kills in 1d6 months, even if the brooch is removed. Each month the victim survives, she loses two points of Constitution. The disease can be eliminated by means of *Cure Disease*, but lost Constitution points do not return.
- Coffer #2 contains 200gp.
- Coffer #3 contains a scroll of *Cure Critical Wounds* inscribed by a 9th-level Cleric.

B7. FROG IDOL

This small cave is empty, except for a large (5' tall) carved stone idol in the shape of a strange being that resembles a frog with fish-like features, such as a dorsal fin and tail. The image has been defaced and cast to the ground, but it is clear that it once was placed in a niche in the wall of the cave.

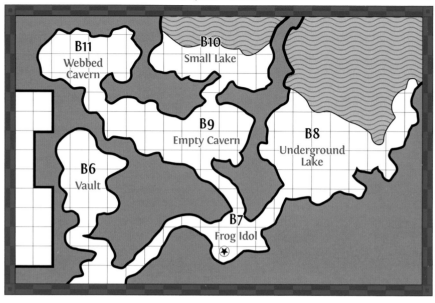

B8. UNDERGROUND LAKE

This large cave is the site of a freshwater lake. Located at the edge of the lake is a stone altar carved with demonic, frog-like images. Its surface is covered with brown stains and there are bone fragments that litter the area surrounding it. When he was alive, Lord Joudain used this altar to summon the lake's inhabitants by offering them sacrifices. The lake is but one small part of a much larger subterranean water system that extends deep beneath the earth.

These creatures take great interest in anything that enters the waters, which is why Joudain entered into a pact with them: in exchange for monthly sacrifices, they would allow him to make use of the water in any way he chose. Anyone else entering the water will find it cold and home to blind cave fish but otherwise benign. The water is quite murky and surprisingly deep—close to 50 feet at its deepest. There is an underwater tunnel that leads down into the depths beneath the chateau. It is immune to Lord Joudain's power and characters could use it to escape if they possess the ability to breathe underwater. Unfortunately, the tunnel goes about a quarter-mile straight down before opening into a large underwater cavern containing an underwater city where the lake's frog-like inhabitants dwell. Referees are free to develop this city as they wish or simply to declare that any characters who travel to it are captured by its inhabitants and never heard from again.

There is a 25% chance that any time the characters enter this cave 1d8 of these creatures will be present. The creatures miss the sacrifices that Lord Joudain provided to them and will thus relish the opportunity to kill more humans. They will gleefully attack any living being they encounter and will pursue them outside the cave if they should flee. The creatures are unaffected by the robe found in the Preparation Room (see p.74).

> **FROG-LIKE CREATURES:** Armor 16, Move 90', 2 Hit Dice, 9hp each, 2 claws for 1d6 damage, 1 bite for 1d4 plus paralysis for 1d6 Turns, Morale 9.

B9. EMPTY CAVERN

This large cavern is completely empty save for some harmless phosphorescent fungi and lichens that give the room an odd greenish glow.

B10. SMALL LAKE

The underground lake found elsewhere also bubbles up into this chamber. Two demonic frogs, gifts to Lord Joudain from the entities dwelling in the lake, lurk here. Being demonic beings, the two frogs do not require earthly sustenance, but they do enjoy the opportunity to kill and maim living beings. They will quickly attack any who enter this cave. The demonic frogs will not attack anyone who enters the chamber wearing the robe found in the Preparation Room (see p.74); their companions, however, are not similarly immune to attack.

> **DEMONIC FROGS:** Armor 14, Move 90', 6 Hit Dice, 39 and 37hp, 1 bite doing 1d10 damage plus poison, Morale 11. Also has a tongue attack that pulls any target toward them when their attack roll against the target is 4 or more higher than needed. Once pulled by the tongue, the target is swallowed and dealt 1d6 points of damage per Round until either the target is dead or she can cut her way out by dealing 6 or more hit points of damage against the Armor 12 stomach.

B11. WEBBED CAVERN

This cavern is filled with large spiderwebs, hanging from what appear to be the desiccated corpses of several humanoid beings. Despite appearances, there are in fact no spiders, giant or otherwise, to be found within this room and the "corpses" are well-crafted mannequins placed here as a jest by Lord Joudain. The mannequins have no value in and of themselves and, other than the tattered clothes they wear, have no possessions. The webs are real and any creature with Strength in the human range can break through them in 2d4 Turns. Creatures of Strength 18 or higher can break through them in 4 Rounds. The strands of the webs are flammable.

1 square = 5 feet

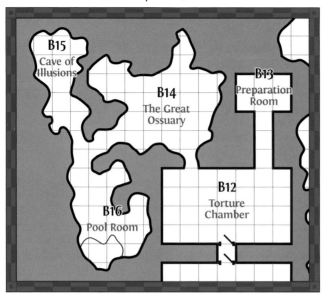

robes, unholy symbols, fetishes, and other similar objects. These date from the days when Lord Joudain toyed with demon worship, hoping it might alleviate his ennui. A few of these objects still remain; all show batrachian themes—frog-like images and shapes abound. None of them are particularly valuable in themselves, although a silver unholy symbol might fetch as much as 100sp to sages or scholars interested in the worship of the obscure demon lord known as Tsath-Dagon in certain grimoires.

B12. TORTURE CHAMBER

This very large chamber is accessible only by means of a locked door, the key to which is in the possession of Landri (Lord Joudain's signet ring also works). The room is filled with all manner of torture devices and implements—racks, branding irons, cages, pillories, etc. Some of these devices are stained with long-dried blood, as are the floors and some of the walls of the room. On one wall, there are a series of hash marks (numbering 117), indicating the number of prisoners who died while in this room decades ago. There are also a number of sketch books that contain drawings of the various tortures put to the unfortunate souls who entered this place.

B13. PREPARATION ROOM

This small chamber's walls are carved from the surrounding stone and contain numerous niches in the walls that once held various ritual paraphernalia, such as

Hanging on a peg in the room is a single greenish-gray hooded robe with a metal clasp in the shape of a frog's head. Anyone wearing the robe will find themselves immune to immediate attack by any frogs or frog-like creatures, whether terrestrial or otherworldly in origin. This immunity extends only to creatures whom the wearer does not attack herself or against whom the wearer does not take violent action. Should she attack a frog, the cloak's effects are nullified.

B14. THE GREAT OSSUARY

This large cavern was used by Lord Joudain and his servants as a repository for the bones of those murdered or sacrificed within the chateau over the years. Even now, his undead servants bring the bones of those slain here to rest within this chamber. Characters who investigate will find that there are a lot of bones here, probably enough to account for several hundred individuals. Lurking amidst the bones is a roiling white ooze created by Lord Joudain through necromantic rituals from bones, skin, and gristle. The ooze is malevolently intelligent and will lie in wait until any living beings come within 10 feet of its resting place in the northeast corner of the cavern, after which it will attack. A careful search amongst the bones will reveal little in the way of treasure except a gold ring (worth 200sp) that contains an inscription, reading "To Petronille."

> **BONE OOZE:** Armor 12, Move 20', 6 Hit Dice, 30hp, 1 slam attack doing 2d4 damage, Morale 12. Attack does an additional 1d6 cold damage on a failed saving throw versus Breath Weapon.

B15. CAVE OF ILLUSIONS

This cave is, like several others, dimly lit by a greenish phosphorescence provided by otherwise harmless fungi and lichens that cover its walls and ceiling. The cave also exudes a faintly sweet odor that is noticeable by any creature who takes the time to smell the air within it. Otherwise, they will not notice the odor.

Regardless of whether they notice the odor, any character who enters the cave must immediately make a saving throw versus Poison (at +2 if they notice the odor and take precautions, such as covering their mouths, etc.) or breathe in a noxious gas that is seeping into the room through a crevice in the western wall of the cave.

Those who fail the saving throw will see an illusion of a horrific creature menacing them. A different creature is visible to each character affected by the gas and all such illusions cannot be seen by anyone else, even those affected by their own illusions. Each Round, the illusory creature attacks (as a 4 Hit Dice monster). If it scores a hit, the target dies from fright. If it fails to score a hit, the target gets another saving throw versus Poison to shake off the effects of the gas. Characters so affected can do nothing but cower in fear until they shake off the effects of the gas, are slain by the illusion, or their unaffected comrades do something to save them. Characters removed from the cavern return to their senses 1 Round after breathing clean air once more. The cave contains nothing else of value.

B16. POOL ROOM

This large cave contains what looks like a pool made from a strange silvery-black metal. The sides of the pool are inscribed with a peculiar writing that defies even magical attempts to decipher it. The pool is completely devoid of any liquid. However, there is a large amount of reddish sediment at its bottom. If examined, the sediment is some type of earth, although not any sort from the area around the chateau— or indeed anywhere on this world. Sages well versed in the lore of other worlds might be able to identify it as hailing from Mars, and suggest that such earth is used as a component in the creation of portals to this alien planet, which is precisely what Lord Joudain did in his quest to alleviate his boredom. The portal could theoretically be recreated here if the characters filled it with water and performed the proper magical rituals, but finding such knowledge might prove difficult, as the tomes that included them are no longer to be found within the chateau.

reference

the household staff

ARNAUD - Land Steward (p.16)

ARNAUD: Armor 12, Move 60', 2 Hit Dice, 12hp, punch 1d8, Morale 12.

BERTRAND - Groom (p.16)

BERTRAND: Armor 12, Move 90', 1 Hit Die, 6hp, 1 claw 1d6, Morale 12.

CLARETA - Chamber Maid (p.17)

CLARETA: Armor 17, Move 150', 4 Hit Dice, 26hp, 1 touch 1d8, Morale 12. Each time a touch deals 6 or more points of damage, the target must make a saving throw versus Magic or lose experience points down to halfway up the previous level. Clareta is incorporeal.

ELIAS - House Steward (p.17)

ELIAS: Armor 12, Move 60', 3 Hit Dice, 18hp, 1 strike 1d8, Morale 12. Elias can absorb up to 8 spell levels cast within 10' of him, negating their effects. Each time he absorbs spell energy in this way, his head grows noticeably larger. After reaching 8 total spell levels, his head explodes, dealing 2d6 damage to all within 10'. If this occurs, Elias is irrevocably destroyed and not even Joudain can restore him to un-life.

ESTÈVE - Valet (p.18)

ESTÈVE: Armor 14, Move 90', 2 Hit Dice, 14hp, two claws 1d4 damage each, Morale 12. Anyone struck by Estève must save versus Paralyzation or be paralyzed for 3d6 Turns.

GUILHÈM - Page (p.18)

GUILHÈM: Armor 15, Move 120', 1 Hit Die, 5hp, 1 punch 1d4, Morale 12. Guilhèm is incorporeal.

HERVISSE - Chef (p.19)

HERVISSE: Armor 12, Move 60', 2 Hit Dice, 13hp, 1 cleaver 1d8, Morale 12.

JAUME AND MIQÈL - 1st and 2nd Footmen (p.19)

JAUME & MIQÈL: Armor 14, Move 90', 3 Hit Dice, 19hp (Jaume), 15hp (Miqèl), 1 punch 1d8, Morale 12.

JULIAN - Gardener (p.20)

JULIAN: Armor 13, Move 60', 2 Hit Dice, 12hp, 1 bite 1d4, Morale 12. Bite causes rotting disease unless treated with holy water; disease permanently removes 1 point of Constitution per week. Julian is incorporeal.

LANDRI - Majordomo (p.20)

LANDRI: Armor 12, Move 60', 3 Hit Dice, 17hp, 1 punch 1d4, Morale 12.

LAURENSA - Parlor Maid (p.21)

LAURENSA: Armor 14, Move 90', 2 Hit Dice, 11hp, two claw attacks 1d4 damage each, Morale 12. Anyone struck by Laurensa must save versus Paralyzation or be paralyzed for 3d6 Turns.

MARTIN - Stable Master (p.21)

MARTIN: Armor 16, Move 60', 3 Hit Dice, 20hp, 42 claw attacks 1d8 each, Morale 12.

MONDETTE - Kitchen Maid (p.22)

MONDETTE: Armor 14, Move 90', 2 Hit Dice, 13hp, 2 claws 1d6 damage each, Morale 12.

RIXENDA - Chamber Maid (p.22)

RIXENDA: Armor 14, Move 90', 2 Hit Dice, 13hp, two claws 1d4 damage each, Morale 12. Anyone struck by Rixenda must save versus Paralyzation or be paralyzed for 3d6 Turns.

YSABEL - Maid (p.23)

YSABEL: Armor 12, Move 90', 5 Hit Dice, 29hp, 1 touch 1d8, Morale 12. Her weeping requires saving throw versus Magic by all within 10 feet of her. Those who fail suffer a random effect (1d6) for the next 5 Rounds: 1. Attack Ysabel; 2. No effect; 3-4. Uncontrollable weeping; 5. Wanders away; 6. Attacks allies. Ysabel is incorporeal.

UNDEAD IMMUNITIES & RESISTANCES

- All of the household staff are undead.
- All can see 60 feet in the dark.
- Immune to all mind-affecting spells (charms, illusions, etc.), as well as poison, *Sleep*, paralysis, stunning, and disease.
- Make no noise unless text states otherwise.
- Corporeal undead immune to "lower half" of all weapon damage dice.
- Incorporeal undead immune to all physical attacks; can only be harmed by spells or other magical effects.

others

WOODEN STATUE - M16 (p.37)

WOODEN STATUE: Armor 16, Move 30', 5 Hit Dice, 29hp, 2 punches for 1d8 damage each, Morale 12.

MINOR ENTITIES OF FLAME - C4 (p.42)

MINOR ENTITIES OF FLAME: Armor 18, Move 120', 4 Hit Dice, 15hp each, 1 attack for 1d6, Morale 12. If an entity comes into contact with a flammable substance—by a successful attack against a cloth-wearing opponent or by being struck by a wooden staff, for example—there is a 3 in 6 chance that this attack will spontaneously generate another minor entity of flame that can attack the next Round.

REANIMATED DOGS - C6 (p.43)

REANIMATED DOGS: Armor 14, 2 Hit Dice, 9hp each, 1 bite for 2d4 damage, Morale 11. Each successful bite also drains 1 point of Strength; lost Strength points return at a rate of 1 per Turn.

ANIMATED FURNITURE - G3 (p.46)

ANIMATED FURNITURE: Armor 14, Move 30', 3 Hit Dice, 20hp each, 1 grab or bite attack for 1d6 damage, Morale 10.

MASS OF PAPERS - G21 (p.55)

MASS OF PAPERS: Armor 12, Move 30', 5 Hit Dice, 32hp, one slam doing 1d6 damage, Morale 12. Any spellcaster struck by the mass must make a saving throw versus Magic or have a single spell of the lowest level she can cast stripped from her mind. This heals the mass by 1d6 per level of the spell. Spells cast at the mass have no effect (except those that produce or mimic fire effects) and increase its hit dice (and hit points) by 1 per spell level. The mass takes double damage from non-magical fire.

AERIAL ENTITY - U6 (p.59)

AERIAL ENTITY: Armor (see below), Move 240', 5 Hit Dice, 29hp, 2 immaterial tentacles for 1d6 damage each, Morale 12. Immune to normal attacks, first attack against creature always misses, vulnerable to silver (takes +1 damage per die).

BAYEMON - U8 (p.61)

BAYEMON: Armor 16, Move 90', 7 Hit Dice, 32hp, 2 claw attacks for 1d6 damage each, 1 bite attack for 1d8 damage plus poison (save or die), Morale 12. Can cast Darkness at will. Any creature slain by the demon cannot be restored to life by any means.

BERNAT - U13 (p.64)

BERNAT: Armor 12, Move 120', 1st Level Fighter, 9hp, 1 fist attack for 1d4 damage, Morale 10.

DAME HELISSENTE - U16 (p.65)

DAME HELISSENTE: Armor 18, Move 150', 6 Hit Dice, 40hp, one ghostly touch attack doing 1d8 damage plus energy drain (see p.25), Morale 12. Usual undead immunities, unaffected by non-magical or non-silver weapons.

FROG-LIKE CREATURES - B8 (p.73)

FROG-LIKE CREATURES: Armor 16, Move 90', 2 Hit Dice, 9hp each, 2 claws for 1d6 damage, 1 bite for 1d4 plus paralysis for 1d6 Turns, Morale 9.

DEMONIC FROGS - B10 (p.73)

DEMONIC FROGS: Armor 14, Move 90', 6 Hit Dice, 39 and 37hp, 1 bite doing 1d10 damage plus poison, Morale 11. Also has a tongue attack that pulls any target toward them when their attack roll against the target is 4 or more higher than needed. Once pulled by the tongue, the target is swallowed and dealt 1d6 points of damage per Round until either the target is dead or she can cut her way out by dealing 6 or more hit points of damage against the Armor 12 stomach.

BONE OOZE - B14 (p.75)

BONE OOZE: Armor 12, Move 20', 6 Hit Dice, 30hp, 1 slam attack doing 2d4 damage, Morale 12. Attack does an additional 1d6 cold damage on a failed saving throw versus Breath Weapon.

joudain's fun

+1 per 2 points of damage suffered by any Player Character (cumulative)

+1 per keyed area explored in the chateau or its grounds

+1 per combat in which the party engages

+1 per failed saving throw by a Player Character

+1 per prohibited spell a Player Character attempts to cast (see Front Gate, p.40)

+1 per attempt to break through the magical barrier with any implement

+1 per member of the household staff encountered

+1 per time a Player Character utters a curse (+2 if she curses God, the saints, etc.)

+1 per time a Player Character verbally expresses fear ("I'm frightened," "This is scary," etc.)

+2 per ability point lost/drained by any means

+2 per failed attempt to use *Turn Undead* on one of the household staff

+5 if the Player Characters present Ysabel with lilacs (see p.36)

+5 if the Player Characters destroy Arnaud or Jaume

+5 per new token left at the grave of Ysabel at area M12 (see p.36)

+10 per act of kindness shown toward Guilhèm or Ysabel

+10 per level drained

+20 per Player Character death

-1 per 1 point of damage healed

-2 per successful saving throw by a Player Character

-2 per time a Player Character exhorts her companions to be brave

-3 per ability point gained/restored by any means

-3 per time a Player Character praises God, the saints, etc.

-4 per successful use of *Turn Undead* on one of the household staff

-5 per attempt to break through a hedge maze wall

-10 per token taken from the grave of Ysabel at area M12 (see p.36)

-10 if the bones of Ysabel at area M12 (see p.36) are in any way disturbed

-15 per level restored by any means

-20 if the characters destroy Guilhèm or Ysabel

-25 per character restored to life by any means

d100 RANDOM EVENT (1-25)

1. A deck of playing cards appears on a nearby table or shelf (or on the ground, if outside). The cards are stained with fresh blood.

2. A character looking into any nearby reflective surface (a mirror, window, water, etc.) sees not her own face but a red-skinned demonic one instead.

3. A statue, painting, or other work of art speaks the name of a random character and tells her, "Flee, while you still can!"

4. The characters hear disembodied cackling coming from behind the closest door or wall.

5. A colony of bats flies about the characters' heads but disappears into thin air before it reaches them.

6. The closest door suddenly swings open with a loud bang. Re-roll if there are no doors nearby.

7. The character briefly feels as if dozens of crawling insects have gotten under her clothing or armor, when in fact no such thing has occurred.

8. The next step a random character takes causes a black slimy substance to bubble out on to the surrounding area from beneath the ground/floor. The slime is not dangerous but it has a noxious odor. This event cannot occur on the upper level of the chateau, in which case nothing happens.

9. One of Lord Joudain's dogs (see p.43) wanders into the area, barks loudly, and then attacks the nearest character.

10. Hervisse (see p.19) walks in the direction of the chateau's kitchen (area L6). He takes no notice of the characters unless they impede his progress in any way.

11. Landri (see p.20) appears and says to the characters, "Can't you follow directions? The stables are that way." He then waits to see that the characters actually leave the chateau (he will open even a magically locked door) before heading toward his room. If the characters do not leave or attack him, he will call for Jaume and Miqèl (see p.19) to deal with them. Re-roll if already outside the chateau.

12. Rixenda (see p.22) crosses the characters' path. She stops to ask if the characters have seen Ysabel, as "the Master wants her." The characters' response to her (including its truthfulness) does not matter and she will head toward the high hall (see area G15) afterward.

13. The character with the lowest Charisma feels herself shoved from behind by an invisible force. She must make a saving throw versus Magic or stumble to the ground, taking no damage.

14. Ysabel (see p.23) can be seen crying in the corner of the area. She will not say anything to the characters and, if approached, will fade out of view.

15. Guilhèm (see p.18) appears. He simply smiles at the characters before proceeding away from them and fading out of view. If attacked or impeded, he calls on Jaume and Miqèl (see p.19) to aid him.

16. The character with the most experience points suddenly notices that an item is no longer on her person. A quick scan of the area reveals that the item is located nearby but with no indication whatsoever as to how it got where it is now.

17. Laurensa (see p.21) and Rixenda (see p.22) both run at the characters, attacking them.

18. Arnaud (see p.16) stomps loudly through the area, heading to Landri's chambers (area G5).

19. Any Clerics present find that their holy symbols have disappeared. The symbols will be found in the next area the characters enter.

20. Bertrand (see p.16) appears, asking the characters to hide him from Martin, who is apparently very upset with the way he has been shirking his duties. If the characters make an effort to help Bertrand, he will disappear shortly afterward. If they do not, he will first plead with them and then fly into a rage and attack them.

21. Jaume (see p.19) appears, offering to show the characters to whatever area they next wish to visit. He refrains from answering most questions, saying "That's not for me to say, madam (or sir)." He will defend himself if attacked but will otherwise not interact with the characters beyond the specific task they have given him.

22. Estève (see p.18) appears and offers to escort the characters to the high hall (area G15), where Laurensa and Rixenda await (assuming they have not been destroyed) to attack and devour them.

23. Clareta (see p.17) moves into view, cleaning and generally straightening the area. She will ask the characters to leave the area until she is done. If they do not comply, she will summon Jaume and Miqèl (see p.19) to handle the matter for her.

24. The door knob of the room turns into a tooth-filled mouth and bites the character who touches it, dealing 1d4 points of damage. If there is no door, nothing happens.

25. Guilhèm comes running at the characters, laughing happily. He simply passes through them before disappearing completely.

d100 RANDOM EVENT (26-48)

26. Miqèl (see p.19) appears, offering to lead the characters into the next area. He will defend himself if he is attacked but will otherwise not interact with the characters beyond the performance of his duties.

27. A spectral hand reaches up and tries to grab the ankle of the character with the lowest Strength. This is successful if the character fails a saving throw versus Paralyzation. The grab deals 1d4 damage and holds the character until she (or another character) attempts to break the hand's hold, after which the hand disperses.

28. A dagger flies at the first character to enter the area. Treat the dagger as a 3rd-level Fighter for determining its chance to hit. If successful, it deals normal damage, after which it is a perfectly normal dagger.

29. Mondette (see p.22) is heading toward the kitchen (area G6). She scowls at the characters as she goes by, but otherwise takes no notice of them. If attacked, she calls on Hervisse (see p.19) to protect her, but he never arrives.

30. If the area has any windows, they audibly crack and shatter, sending shards flying everywhere. The shards deal 1d6 damage to anyone within 5 feet who fails a saving throw versus Breath Weapon. Should the characters ever return to this room, the window will no longer be broken.

31. Landri (see p.20) appears, carrying a book in one hand. He gives the book to one of the characters, saying, "The Master wants you to read this before dinner this evening" before he departs. The book is, however, completely blank.

32. The characters hear a female voice say, "I thought you didn't like uninvited guests."

33. The closest nearby fireplace suddenly roars to life. The flames are real and last until they run out of fuel (1d4 Turns) or they are extinguished. If there are no fireplaces nearby, re-roll.

34. The character with the lowest Constitution score levitates 2 feet off the ground for the number of Rounds by which her score is lower than 13, after which she simply falls to the ground. If all the characters' Constitution scores are 13 or greater, nothing happens.

35. The area is affected by magical spiderwebs that require 2d4 Turns to cut through, though flames will destroy them in 2d4 Rounds.

36. Jaume (see p. 19) walks into view, smiling and muttering to himself, "It was still worth it." If no one attacks him or impedes him, he will continue to walk away.

37. Miqèl (see p.19) wanders into the area, clutching his split head and moaning through his bifurcated mouth. He completely ignores the characters unless they attack him or otherwise impede his movement.

38. The lowest-level character is pushed from behind. She must make a successful saving throw versus Paralyzation or fall to the ground.

39. A voice can be heard whispering the words to the "Our Father" in Latin but backwards.

40. Bertrand (see p.16) is found sleeping in the next area. If he is awakened, either on purpose or by making loud noises, he will be fly into a rage and attack the characters.

41. The shadow of the character with the lowest Charisma score begins to notice-ably distort and take on other shapes, including that of a horned demon, before it returns to its original shape.

42. An insubstantial cat crosses in front of the characters' path before disappearing. The first character to walk beyond where the cat appeared suffers a -1 penalty on her next saving throw.

43. A bag of 100sp appears on the floor.

44. Mondette (see p.22) appears and begins to flirt with the male character with the highest Charisma. 1d4 Rounds later, Hervisse (see p.19) will appear and attack the object of Mondette's affections. She will join in this attack with glee.

45. Fresh flowers are found in a vase on a table or shelf in the area.

46. Julian (see p.20) clomps loudly through the area. His spectral shoes appear to be covered in mud, which he tracks onto the ground. Shortly after he steps forward, he looks down, notices the mess he is making and curses to himself. He looks at the characters and says, "The Master will not like this one bit" before disappearing.

47. Hervisse (see p.19X) enters the area, armed with a cleaver. He asks the characters if they have seen Mondette and "that bastard." If they hesitate to answer or question him, he begins to accuse them of "trying to hide the truth from me," after which he attacks.

48. A water-damaged book is found. The book is missing many pages and the handwriting inside is often smeared. However, it is clearly Joudain's journal. The legible pages (all of which are near the end) talk about Joudain's looking forward to seeing the latest pair of peasants whom Martin (see p.21) has brought to the chateau. He hopes that they might prove useful in his experiments.

d100 RANDOM EVENT (49-70)

49. Guilhèm (see p.18) wanders around nearby, as if searching for something. He is missing one of his shoes and asks the characters if they have seen it. If they have (see entry 78) and can direct him toward its location (or, better yet, give it to him), he will reward them by answering truthfully any one question they have about the chateau. The Referee should bear in mind that Guilhèm has the mind of a child and Joudain shielded him from many of the worst aspects of the place.

50. A piece of crumpled paper appears on the ground. If read, it is revealed to be a page from Joudain's journal in which he rants at length about his boredom and how he wishes to be entertained. He then lists several mundane activities in which he has recently engaged that he hoped might do so—reading, going riding, visiting a nearby town, etc.—but that have failed to hold his attention. He then intimates that he might need to look elsewhere for diversion.

51. Elias (see p.17) calls to the characters from behind the closest door, asking them to unlock it. The characters will find the door unlocked, despite Elias's claims. If the door is opened, he thanks the characters before heading away from them, muttering about how he will have to report Jaume and Miqèl's tomfoolery to the Master. If there are no doors nearby, nothing happens.

52. Clareta (see p.17) offers the characters some sweets from a bag that she pulls from her apron. If the characters do not accept her offer, she attacks them. If they do accept, she will wait until one or more of them has consumed the sweets before leaving. Each character who consumes one must make a saving throw versus Poison. Those who fail suffer nausea for the next 1d4 Turns, which exacts a -2 penalty on all attack rolls and saving throws. Those who succeed gain a +2 bonus to the same rolls for the same duration.

53. Any Player Characters slain in the chateau thus far are reanimated, as described on p.25. (Repeatable)

54. Nothing happens—the Player Characters get lucky this time. (Repeatable)

55. Lord Joudain briefly manifests as a ghostly apparition of himself as a child (see area G17 for a description), points at a random character, and laughs before he fades away. (Repeatable)

56. The characters hear a loud creaking noise, either beneath their own feet or above their heads, as appropriate. (Repeatable)

57. The characters hear a woman scream. (Repeatable)

58. Fresh blood drips from a nearby wall and pools on the floor. (Repeatable)

59. A broom, rake, shovel, or other similar implement springs to life briefly and smacks a nearby character on the head. The implement has Armor 13, 1 Hit Die, 5 hit points, deals 1 point of damage per hit and continues until it is destroyed. (Repeatable)

60. A skeleton assembles out of a nearby pile of bones and attacks the characters. The skeleton has Armor 14, 1 Hit Die, 4hp, and does 1d4 damage. (Repeatable)

61. Lord Joudain briefly manifests as a ghostly apparition of himself as an adult (see area G17 on the ground level for a description), stares intently at a random character and sighs deeply, before he fades away. (Repeatable)

62. The characters see glowing red eyes in the nearest darkened area. The eyes fade from view as soon as the characters get within 10 feet of them. (Repeatable)

63. A number of dancing, purplish lights appear and briefly circle about the characters before winking out of existence. (Repeatable)

64. The character with the lowest Wisdom hears her name whispered in her right ear. (Repeatable)

65. A nearby piece of furniture (or statue or bush) moves a couple of inches along the floor. (Repeatable)

66. A candle, chandelier, lantern, or other light source in the room lights itself up and remains illuminated for 1d10 Rounds before extinguishing. (Repeatable)

67. Lord Joudain briefly manifests as a ghostly apparition of himself as a youth (see area G17 on the ground level for a description), and lunges at a random character with a spectral sword, which passes right through her, before he fades away. (Repeatable)

68. A scratching sound emanates from a nearby wooden wall panel. The sound stops as soon as the characters get close to it. (Repeatable)

69. Any sources of illumination the characters are carrying (torches, lanterns, etc.) flicker for a moment and then go out. (Repeatable)

70. The character with the fewest experience points feels something move past her feet, like an animal. Looking down, she sees nothing. (Repeatable).